Silence is my homeland

Published in association with The National Writers Club

---

*Winner of The National Writers Club
Award for Nonfiction*

A Stackpole/Cameron House Book

Gilean Douglas

Silence
is my
homeland

Life on Teal River

Illustrations by Stephanie Scott Brown

SILENCE IS MY HOMELAND
Copyright © 1978 by
Gilean Douglas
Winner of The National Writers Club Award for Nonfiction

Published by
STACKPOLE BOOKS
Cameron and Kelker Streets
P.O. Box 1831
Harrisburg, Pa. 17105
in association with The National Writers Club

Published simultaneously in Don Mills, Ontario, Canada
by Thomas Nelson & Sons, Ltd.

Printed in the U.S.A.

Library of Congress Cataloging in Publication Data

Douglas, Gilean.
  Silence is my homeland.

  1. Natural history—British Columbia. 2. Outdoor
life—British Columbia. 3. Douglas, Gilean.
4. Naturalists—British Columbia—Biography. I. Title.
QH106.2.B8D68   1978   500.9′711   78-2324
ISBN 0-8117-1521-3

*This book is for Dorothy,
Audrey, Elsie and Susan*

BY THE SAME AUTHOR

Now the Green Word, Prairie Press
The Pattern Set, Prairie Press
Poetic Plush, Prairie Press
Seascape with Figures, Prairie Press
Now in This Night, Prairie Press
River for My Sidewalk, J. M. Dent & Sons (Canada) Ltd
Modern Pioneers (editor), Mitchell Press
The Protected Place, Gray's Publishing Ltd (forthcoming)

Short extracts from this book have been published in the *Victoria Colonist, Saturday Night, The Country Guide, Montreal Star, Forest and Outdoors, Canadian Mining Journal, Vancouver Sun, Trails, The Improvement Era, Literary Florida, The Land, Front Rank, The Young People, United Publications,* and *The Villager.* Thanks are extended to these publications.

Contents

1   HOME   *9*

2   THE BLOSSOMING   *23*

3   SUN IN THE VALLEY   *38*

4   THE PILGRIMAGE   *47*

5   COMMISSIONER OF TRAILS   *60*

6 HIGH MOUNTAINS ARE A FEELING   *79*

7 NOW IN SEPTEMBER   *106*

8 END AND BEGINNING   *124*

9 WILDERNESS WINTER   *145*

SOURCES FOR QUOTATIONS   *158*

1

Home

Let the fields and the gliding streams in the valleys delight me. Inglorious, let me court the rivers and forests.
VIRGIL

For more than twenty years I had been homeless. It was not that I had no roof over my head during that time, but that I had too many. Roofs of relatives' houses, schools, boardinghouses, apartments, duplexes, tents, automobiles, trains, ships, summer cottages. But there had never been a home. I had watered plants in pots and window boxes; I had sprayed other people's roses or dug around dejected annuals in tiny plots beside brick walls. Once there had even been a minute vegetable corner where carrots, radishes and lettuce put up a gallant battle against wornout and undernourished soil. But there had never been a garden. Not a *real* garden.

Then one day as I was fishing a strange western river, I came to a deep pool where the steelhead and brook trout were both wise and wary. I flicked a red admiral across the dark green water, hoping for a Dolly Varden, and then I looked up at my surroundings. My right arm dropped slowly to my side, and the top of my rod broke the surface of the pool. I stood perfectly still and was not conscious that I breathed, for there, right across from me, gazing into my face with its deep-set windows, was — my home.

A little river bounced down through mountain passes to join, just east of the pool, the larger river I had been following. The little river was the Wren; its companion, the Teal. Together they formed two sides of a rectangle of which the third was a high wooded mountain — very appropriately called Evergreen — and the fourth a forest. Within this rectangle lay a clearing of perhaps two acres with a cabin in the center and three smaller outbuildings nearby. The whole was a plateau raised some fifty feet above water level and covered with wild berry bushes and large stumps.

Fording the river below the pool, I went on a reconnaissance tour. Yet I knew before I climbed the short, steep bank to the clearing that this was the house in which I was going to live, that this underbrush was the vegetable field I was going to cultivate. When the heavy nail-studded door of fir swung open upon the musty and dark interior of the cabin, I was already seeing visions. That was, indeed, almost all I could see. There were eleven windows in the three rooms with, by a miracle, only two panes broken, but they were all too grimy to admit more than a mulatto twilight. Everything was incredibly dirty, and the air was high with mold and mouse. The cedar paneling of walls and ceiling was hung with cobweb tapestry and the rough fir floor — there is, unfortunately, no hardwood of any size in the vicinity — looked as if it might be several inches lower when it was scraped and scrubbed.

But in less than half an hour all that was changed. There was a corner bunk in the bedroom with an attached table at the side and book shelves that were built into the foot. A lampstand nestled above in the angle of the wall, with another to balance it in the diagonal corner. A built-in desk and cupboards filled the other corners, while two chairs — already in residence — and a small table under one of the windows completed the furnishings.

The living-room also had a built-in bunk, desk and lampstands. There was a cupboard opposite the stone fireplace and a large bookcase in one of the walls, just where firelight with its pagan art would illuminate the bindings. Butterbox chairs and a drop-leaf table — also in residence and made by better carpenters than my neighbors and I turned out to be — were placed on the dark brown floor covered with hand-hooked rugs; homespun curtains contrasted with the white — or

perhaps red — window-trim. Another door, half glass, opened onto a small front porch with a green roof and a gay red floor. And yes — I almost forgot — there was also a new door in the bedroom, opening onto a grassy terrace where summer meals could be flavored by sun and wind.

The kitchen had a drop-leaf table and several built-in cupboards in addition to the cabinet, stove and water pail table already there. Chinese blue and lacquer red answered the cabin's cry for color, and gay wooden plaques brightened the satin cedar walls. Outside, my little home looked as though it had sprung from the very soil on which it stood. An eaved green roof contrasted with the reddish tinge of the hemlock bark walls, and blossoming green window boxes pictured themselves against white trim. Bordered stone paths and flowerbeds were everywhere in the clearing, but there was nothing straight or formal — nothing that could not live with the lovely inconsequence of forest, river and mountain.

Yes, after half an hour on that August morning, it was exactly like that. It was — and almost is. But the reality came only after several months and considerable assistance. For I was no carpenter. Neither was I a gardener — although I attended to all that part myself — or anything very much except, perhaps, a writer. I had been accustomed all my life to comfort flowing from gadgets that one pushed or pulled; to electricity, plumbing (of course I *did* have running water — in the rivers) and all the many contraptions — with an accent on the "trap" — which we of this century feel we cannot live without. But I did not miss them. I sloughed off civilization as one doffs a coat that is too tight and found that I had never been so comfortable before.

I will admit, however, that the board situation was a trifle startling to one who had been accustomed to lumber yards at the other end of a telephone. Here you go out and catch a likely looking cedar tree and imitate George Washington. You saw the best parts of it into six-foot lengths and then, with the aid of a froe, a sledge hammer and considerable profanity, you split off shakes — known as boards "outside" — of the desired thickness. One of those unforgettable moments comes when you discover that the interior of your tree has as many waves as a permanent or is as knotty as a rheumatic gaffer. Then you count ten, say it anyway and begin all over.

Of course it is not necessary to cut down a tree when there is a good one on the ground. If it had been, my cabin would have gone shakeless forever. Neither is it necessary to use cedar, but the wood is both light and enduring, great assets when you are transport, sawmill and furniture factory all in one. When you have carried the boards home on your sturdy shoulders, you plane them for hours and hours until they are as smooth as a politician's manner. After that you keep them polished and receive congratulations.

But I had no need of congratulations, for to me those hours of planning and polishing were filled with happiness. Those boards were part of me and of my home as they never could have been if I had bought them from a sawmill. Why, they had grown on my land; they had felt the same cool wind that came down from the uplands in summer. They were related to those very trees that had been felled to build part of my cabin in 1860 and to finish it fifteen years ago. There had been another cabin nearby in the gold-rush days, but it had evidently been wiped out by fire for I discovered the charred foundation logs when I was putting in the big rock garden and steps beside the patch leading downhill to the Teal. Another ancient cabin — a small one of logs — still stands on the other side of the Wren just below Cougar mountain. Most of my good leaf mold has come from there, for erosion and the many deciduous trees have combined to produce a rich soil. But the old prospectors who built the cabin thought even less of comfort than I, for the whole affair is only about the size of my bedroom, with just space enough for a palsied cedar shake bunk, a stool and a small table on which the stove stood, although cooking was also done over a stone fireplace outside. There is no window at all, and the whole gives an impression of a den rather than of a dwelling.

My reconnaissance that first August showed me that my own soil was fairly good, although baked hard by the summer sun. A few gallant sweet williams struggled up through it, and there were enough wild berry bushes to satisfy even the most ardent fruit eater. Of course they needed pruning badly, and in many places the forest was beginning to take its own back again. Some attempt had evidently been made at a vegetable garden at one time, and there were weedy flowerbeds around the house. I have been able to learn very little about those who occupied the cabin before me, but their handiwork tells me that they cared enough to put time and thought and patient craft into it, and for that I am glad. A place that has been loved, even a little, is a good place to live. Loving and living go together.

So that September I moved in. "It is a comfortable feeling to know that you stand on your own ground. Land is about the only thing that can't fly away." The woodshed was half-full of fir, alder, maple, cedar and hemlock, while strawberry plants and wildflowers covered the clearing. I could hardly wait to obey Thoreau and begin to put foundations under my castle in the air. Of my little domain I could feel: "However small it is on the surface, it is four thousand miles deep, and that is a very handsome property."

It was the great moment of my life when I waded the Teal River with my packboard on my back and stood at last on my own ground. I can never describe the feeling that surged up inside me then. I stood now where I should have been always. I felt kinship in everything around me, and the long city years of noise and faces were just fading photographs. What it meant to me to walk in my own door and know that all this was mine — mine — I cannot put in words. I kept touching things: flowers, furniture, even the piled wood as though they were all my children, my children whom I loved very much. My heart sang every moment and I was impatient with sleep.

September and October were golden months. Gradually the slopes of Fireweed — the fire-scarred mountain on the north side of the Teal — and Cougar mountain showed yellow and crimson, and even Evergreen betrayed glowing touches here and there against the steady darkness of its conifers. The days were warm sunshine and the cool nights glinted with silver. The water in the rivers began to rise, but before it was too high for wading I had rejuvenated — again with considerable assistance — the cables across each stream and repaired the cages to ride in. Before the November rains arrived, the woodshed was filled, an acre of land dug over, a fair amount of bush cleared and my roof mended. The larger stumps had to remain, but I partially hollowed them out and filled them with earth for spring flowers.

My pride in everything would have amused an outsider. Between writing, carpentering and warming the house against the snows of that first winter, I worked twelve to fourteen hours a day — and even that workload was not enough to satisfy me. Everything I did was joyful. It was, perhaps, just as well for my life of freedom that no one saw me gloating over my handiwork or going outside to talk to the great Douglas fir which had become my particular friend! I could not explore my domain enough or look too often at the magnificent views that soothed my eyes like sleep. It was impossible to decide which season was the loveliest.

There is no season such delight can bring,
As summer, autumn, winter, and the spring.

Watching each season go was like parting from a loved companion, but my sorrow was never too great or I should not have been able to welcome properly the comrade just arriving.

Putting my first seeds into the ground was a revelation. I felt as though the skies had opened and shown me a vision of life as it should be. When I was actually eating my own vegetables and fruits, with my own flowers on the table, I would not have changed places with anyone in the world. How I pitied city people — of whom I had been one such a short time before. With even their air filtered for them, what artificial and sterile lives they led. How could they ever get down to the vital root of things, separated as they were from the good earth by brick and stone? Surely they also were separated from much of the life force and from the curative powers of earth.

So spring, with violets and trilliums flowering in my woods, flowed into summer. The soft, cool air changed to warm winds and rainless dust. I was up at dawn to work among my vegetables and flowers before the sun was on them, and in the evening I would carry up pails from the Wren for watering. It was the following year before ram, tank and troughs were put in to solve the acute irrigation problem.

I discovered that my cabin was close to four east-west and two north-south trails, but that these forest highways were only for pedestrians or pack horses. Everything had to be brought in on human backs or on those of broncos — if one possessed the latter luxury. I had known from the beginning that my nearest neighbor was three miles away and that my only link with "outside" would be the small branch railway that toddled along the slope of Fireweed mountain. My neighbors considered themselves very fortunate that they were so much closer to the railroad than I, while I was delighted that I was so much farther off from it than they. They were convinced that I was very wrong to feel as I did in this matter, while I had no thoughts at all on the subject as it concerned them. There was far too much else to think about that first year. At any time Jeremy Taylor has my full endorsement when he says: "Every man hath in his own life sins enough, in his own mind trouble enough; so that curiositie after the affairs of others cannot be without envy and an evil minde. What is it to me if any Neighbour's Grandfather were a Syrian, or his Grandmother illegitimate, or that another is indebted five thousand pounds, or whether his wife be expensive?"

But when the wind is blowing from the north, it is pleasant to awaken in the night and hear the far-off whistle of the train as it picks its way along the mountainside with a sheer drop of two or three hundred feet below it. There is one engine that is very blasé about it all, and its toots for dangerous curves — of which there are many — are decidedly perfunctory. But when a new engine is on the line, then what wailing and caterwauling! The prairie engines, which are suddenly transferred to this mountain run, practically have nervous breakdowns, and it is quite heartrending to hear their plaintive tootles, which sound as though they were being whipped into going ahead at all.

Most of the forest along the Teal River has been timbered off, but up the Wren fire has been the only devastator as it is too arduous an undertaking to get the logs out and up to the railroad. A shingle mill operated not far away until twelve years ago, and the first sawmill went in at the same time as the gold hunters. Pole cutters have been through at various periods and now there are very few really large trees left standing. On my land, before I came, a fir nearly seven feet in diameter was felled simply for boards and firewood — and three fourths of it is still lying there. Such signs of vandalism — and there are many of them — make me glad that I could rescue at least a few acres and save such friends as my big Douglas fir (over four hundred years old and with his bark worn off by mountain lions for more than seven feet around the base) from destruction.

I did not learn all these things in that first spring and summer, but I came tentatively to know my immediate surroundings and particularly Home Wood, the fourth side of my rectangle. I also came to know my immediate neighbors: furred, feathered and finned. One summer night I walked out the kitchen door to find Mrs. Barrow's Goldeneye Duck waddling happily up the path from the Wren. She and I became very friendly indeed, and I was glad that I was there to cluck my tongue sympathetically when she told me the sad tale of a husband who spent most of the summer basking at the seaside, leaving her to bring up the family alone.

One of my weekend guests was unusually interesting. I heard that a bird — what kind no one seemed to know — had been shot near the railroad and that its mate was there still — and alive. That was enough. In a very short while he was reposing on my very young front lawn while I tried to examine the injuries I was sure he must have. But Gussie the grebe refused to cooperate. His black crest went up, his eyes shot fire and his beak snapped with plain and angry intent. He had spent at least four days beside the railroad track — well over a mile, by the shortest route, from his native element — with nothing to eat and with the trains thundering by only a few feet away. But his spirit was magnificently intact. If he had injuries, originally, I could detect nothing now. I kept him that Sunday afternoon and night until I was convinced that he had suffered no damage, then I let him go, for it was impossible for me to obtain enough of his favorite foods and, besides, my lawn (or my cabin at night) was definitely no place for such a warrior.

When we came to the river I held Gussie in my hands for a few moments and then placed him on the water. He flashed underneath it and then appeared again several yards away. He floated down toward Dubh Glas, the big pool of Teal River, and held himself there against the current while he looked anxiously upstream. Perhaps he thought that he might find his mate again if he could make his way through that white water. Finally he seemed to make up his mind that she must have gone downstream ahead of him to the larger Mallard River. I watched him until a bend hid him from view and I was sorry to see him go. Gussie was a rare spirit. It would have been pleasant to have had a few words with the man who was so ready with his gun.

So then it was fall again and I had been in my house a year. Asters were blooming in my garden and their wild brothers brightened the hills and river banks. Smoke from my chimney mingled with the blue haze which drifted over forest and mountain while the rivers sang softly in those days before the floods of autumn. Wren and Alaska robin chirped and called; squirrels were very active and noisy. The Canada jays began to prepare for winter, and so did I. Soon the snow would come swirling down the canyon and through the woods and I must be ready for it.

Those woods had seemed a dark, mysterious place in the beginning, but now they were more familiar to me than any street in any city I had ever known — and I had known many. The graveled paths among my flowers and vegetables were friendly ways also, and even the outland trails were not strange any more. In that second fall the mists of Evergreen mountain so duplicated the smoke streaming from my chimney that I would wonder what campfire was lighted there and what wanderer sat beside it. When the moon appeared after nights of rain, I could not bear to be indoors. Everything must wait. The fire went out, and my supper chilled while I walked beside the rivers with the moon in my face. If I had not shared such moments with those among whom I dwelt, I would have felt myself an alien thing and not worthy of this high living.

Often it seemed that I lived between two worlds, for from the knoll in front of the cabin I could see Fireweed looming darkly above the Teal with mist concealing the fire-wracked slopes and clouds muffling the peaks; then I would turn directly around to find, between Cougar and Evergreen, a half-moon riding bright in a clear sky and the earth transmuted into a fairyland where no darkness could ever come. Even my clothesline became a thing of beauty, strung along its length with crystal moisture like a necklace of the moon. Sometimes the lamplight ran up almost to the top of the tall, straight trees of Home Wood, changing them into vast organ pipes with the rivers for their music.

To many my valley would seem a strange and lonely place, plunged down between dark mountains and shadowed by the darker forest. The sun never shines on its snow, except that of late February and March, and the great rains of spring and autumn shorten light and warmth still more. Winds come shrieking down through the passes, the rivers shout menacingly in flood and, during most of the year, two steel cables are my only connecting link with the outside world. Without them I would have two days' walk over the mountains before I could reach a settlement on my own side of the Teal. But what of all that? An hour's walk will bring the sun when, in December and January, the great longing for it comes. The cables and the tall trees to which they are attached will last, I hope, for my lifetime. I have no radio, no near neighbors — but I have more than these could ever give one.

Never any more to hurry, never to appear what I was not, never to be constrained by the crowd.

Because there is "nothing too much" anywhere, life in my valley takes on zest and adventure as naturally as life in a city clothes itself in conformity and boredom. If I do not grow and prepare food, I starve; if I do not cut firewood, I freeze. It is as simple as that. There is always a feeling of being close to great events. If I become ill, I must cure myself — or die. If I am caught in a rockslide on one of my mountain rambles, if I fall into the swift, icy river of winter — then I shall see death come quickly. It is possible to meet a mountain lion on almost any trail, or even a grizzly who has drifted over from the eastern mountains. Fire lurks in the ever-present oil lamps and among the dry brush of summer and early fall. Any September I may see it tearing the heart out of a tall fir or devouring a stand of hemlock in gulping crunches.

Each day brings new problems and the need for keen wits with which to tackle them. I can never stand at my door on any morning and say: "I know how this day will be." I have lived in strange countries and in equally strange places of my own land, but not one of them has ever given me that sense of achievement and high adventure that I have found here. And "here" is so very small. The journeys I hope we shall take together in these pages will go only four miles west, two north, seven east, perhaps twelve south, eight thousand feet up and a spade's depth down. Such a little space to hold so much. But perhaps, "after we have made the just reckoning which retirement will help us to make, we shall begin to think the world in part measure mad and that we have been in a sort of bedlam all this time."

It is true that a little of this land is in my name and it is also true that I have used the words "my" and "mine" several times in referring to it — and shall probably do so on many more occasions. But they are not used in the ordinary interpretation of possession, for I have never felt that I "owned" anything here. It is mine only in the sense that it is part of me as I am of it. How foolish it would be to say I possessed something that can never be possessed, that has been here centuries before I came and will be here centuries after I am gone. I am only a transient tenant who wished to find, for a pinprick of eternity, succor and serenity; who wished to praise beauty and to share great living.

Whatever comes I shall have had this. I shall have known what it is to work with my hands and brain on my own land and for my own sustenance. I shall have known what it is to work for the community by labor traded back and forth and by supplying vegetables. I shall have known what it is to live completely alone with nature, for sometimes a whole winter will go by without a single human visitor. That is very good. It means that I can learn to know myself and to live with myself, that I can discover the ways of silence and beauty. There are long thoughts then and, I believe good ones, when

The soul selects her own society, Then shuts the door.

It is not the world that is shut out, but its clamor and impatience. Here, with my ear pressed close to the earth, I can listen to the very heart of humanity beating. From my primitive position I can evaluate civilization more truly and, freed from the pointless hurry and distraction of modern society, can appreciate for the first time the delicate nuances of living. The four freedoms

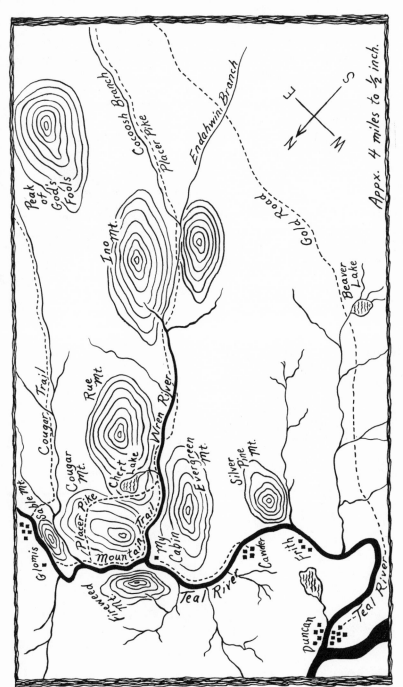

Teal River and Vicinity

are mine, but more than that I have a freedom of spirit that goes beyond and above them, a freedom that comes only when the soul has found itself.

I am not the same person who waded across the Teal that first August morning. I am the wind that comes down from the high hills; I am the deep forest, the singing rivers, the tall mountains. I am all of these things and more; I am the whole human being which they have made me.

Henceforth I ask not good fortune; I, myself am good fortune.
Henceforth I whimper no more, postpone no more, need nothing.

It is not even I who am writing these words now. I am only the means by which they are put down. The Spirit that is behind all the beauty of the world is the real author of this book. If there is failure in it, it is because the instrument is not yet clear and true enough.

2

The blossoming

Jam laeto turgent in palmite gemmae
(Now the buds swell on the joyful stem)

VIRGIL

Each season has its own niche in our hearts and one is not lovelier than another, but spring has a special, secret place. All the bittersweet nostalgia of the past is in it, all present desire, all longing for the future.

It begins when the first seed catalogue arrives. Arabis and forget-me-nots spread along the borders of the beds where delphinium, matricaria and lychnis bloom in patriotic splendor. Gentian, mesembryanthemum and verbena peek from the crevices of the rocks, while the edges of a path riot with white and yellow alyssum. For there are no failures in a catalogue. The purple of kohlrabi, the yellow of corn and the tender green of asparagus sparkle through its pages, and victory over the insect world is a simple and a settled thing.

In February the first seeds go into the brown soil of the many flats, forerunners of those that will be planted soon in garden and vegetable plot. An earth-scented wind blows down from the uplands and it is warm enough to work outside in slacks and shirt, although the sun only stays for a morning hour in the valley. In the woods the snow is still too deep and soft for comfortable walking, but in the clearings where the frost has had its way, one can go anywhere on the white, crisp surface or place a chair on top of it for sun and moonlight basking. The ice bridge in Wren River has broken and the exposed rocks no longer resemble high-risen loaves of bread. The chef caps of the stumps are dwindling and on the elderberry bushes the green buds show plump and hard. Clear drops of melted frost glitter on the evergreens when the sunlight slants through them. Fireweed mountain is as much brown as white, and the afternoon sun creeps farther and farther across the Teal toward the cabin. The dipper's clear song can be heard beside the water and the squirrels shrill again in the woods. The nights, with moonlight cold upon the algid snow, are like any nights of winter, but one could never be mistaken; it is spring.

I know it as I step out of the cabin in the early morning, when the sun is still loitering behind Cougar mountain and the land is gray and cold except for a warm golden band widening slowly down from the top of Evergreen. The air is more zestful, more satisfying than any wine. Taking it into the lungs in chilly, clear breaths is like drinking mountain water that has been cooled in snow and mellowed by a close, cloudless sun until it is a draught of life itself. Pure air and pure water; there is nothing like them. Nothing so satisfying, nothing so invigorating. They cannot take the place of food, but they can so increase its benefits that it nourishes us as it never could otherwise. But they must be drawn into our very being until they permeate and fill us with their purity. Then the mind feels as though a cool stream were running slowly and softly over it, slaking the fever of people and events, seeping into the crevices of each thought and soothing it to peace.

Body and brain become rested and pliant, and there is nothing now that the heart would not attempt. It is a new morning, a new world and I am a newborn soul, seeing it and myself for the first time. Always for the first time, I can never say of any hour of any day: I have met you before, or of any leaf or flower: I have seen you somewhere. When my last hour comes I shall never know it, for I shall still believe that it is my first.

In March I discover the feelings of a baked Alaska pudding as I sit in my chair on top of the hard snow crust and become thoroughly browned. The snow is like plush then and the sun rises higher each day until finally, about the middle of the month, it clears the top of Evergreen and I have its warmth from ten in the morning to three in the afternoon. Surely the sun worshippers came from a land like this rather than from one of perpetual warmth and light. Three months without the sun, as is true here, and anyone would be prepared to swear that he is a a veritable god with miracles at his fingertips. Under him the snows melt away, the rivers rise in flood, trees that seemed dead are quickened to bud and leaf and the iron earth softens so that flowers may clamber through — what greater wonders could there be than these?

But the snow melts very slowly, and it is difficult not to become impatient for the turned earth and transplantings of spring. Odd jobs, such as felling dead or rotting trees, are done this month for there is little else that can be accomplished outdoors. Each night the thermometer on the side porch goes down to sixteen or eighteen above zero, but with the arrival of the sun it springs up to forty or over, only returning to its backsliding ways when the cabin is in shadow again. During this interval the stream that courses down Fireweed mountain becomes a waterfall, but by night it is frozen into immobility once more. These are the nights when the cougars pass within a hundred or so yards of the cabin, their great clawed prints showing clearly on the smooth, hard surface of the snow. This silent, sinuous beast has many names — panther, puma, mountain lion, Mexican lion — but here he has only one. The cougars and the coyotes are the most numerous large inhabitants of the mountains, the bears exceeding them only at berry time.

Toward the middle of March the winds begin, and one day I feel that the strong breeze has lost the edge of winter and that soon the brown earth will be waiting to receive my seed. If I should be put down in a strange place, not knowing what season it was, and a March wind came by I would recognize it immediately. There is a scent in it that is in no other wind and a freedom and freshness about it that can belong to only one month of the year. The wind of each season has its own special perfume and character, and one can never be mistaken for another. The summer wind smells of flowers and cut grass; the autumn wind of smoke and fog and bracken; the winter wind of snow, crisp air and sharp, clean space. But the spring wind has running water in it and the pungent scent of damp earth and

wet bark — and something else that is simply spring and that is all it is.

One morning I find that the ground has not frozen during the dark hours and there is a moistured softness in the air. The snow melts swiftly and more swiftly and the rivers begin to shout. They become faster and wilder and spread out toward their farthest banks in lunges of strong current. Driftwood piles up in every catch place, and my island in the Teal adds something like a hundred feet of logs and gravel to its length. The Wren floods almost to the top of the irrigation sluice boxes, and I can fill my pails by simply bending over the bank. There is no beach left. At night the wind gives my little house a great push from the south and then, suddenly veering, a gigantic shove from the northwest. A window — fortunately a removable one! — blows in across my bed, the door to the living room bangs shut and the rugs are lifted from the floor. Hail and then rain slash down upon the roof, and in the morning streamers of mist lie along the mountains and

The levelled lances of the rain
At earth's half-shielded breast take glittering aim.

When the mists dissolve, fresh snow is seen on the mountain tops, and the downpour changes from gray to white and then back to gray once more. March is as loath as I to say farewell to winter, although just as eager to welcome spring. The snow line drops lower and lower on the mountains, and I feel as though November had come again and the cold months of darkness were still ahead. One morning I wake up to find big, soft flakes fluttering down, and for a week or two everything is as it was before. The nights are sharp with frost and a March moon rides clear and full. The freshly fallen snow has made everything so bright outside that it is possible to read average-size print, and the smoke from my chimney is reflected so strongly that it seems to be the very vapor itself which is drifting, dark and silent, across the white ground and weaving through the bare brown bushes.

Then one morning onion, lettuce and tomato peep greenly through their brown coverings in the flats, while iberis and carnation put up frail shoots toward the light. The big cherry branch that I brought home from a neighbor's pruning opens delicate white blossoms, and suddenly my window is a Chinese print come to life. I take the lovely thing out to photograph it with the snow as background (white against white, but with attention to light, shadow and printing the effect can be very interesting) and then watch it day by day unfold more beauty. Spring has come to be my house guest.

Now the rains begin again, this time in earnest. The mountains are swathed from head to foot in gray mist that, in its moments of lifting, shows creeks cascading from the heights in silver spray. The mournful two-noted call of the varied thrush (called "rainpiper" by my neighbors) sounds from the woods and as he is supposed to be the prophet of downpours, I am sure he must be delighted with the result. Then one afternoon, while the snow is still deep on the ground, I hear doleful cheepings and look out to see Mr. Western Robin declaiming passionately on the subject of food and housing. He has come twenty miles from the village to inform me that if I insist on having snow up here at this outrageous time he simply cannot nest on my property as usual. Thereupon he promptly departs and I am desolate, but with a hope that the plump cranberries and tasty seeds he devoured in the feeding station may tempt him back again.

A flock of Oregon juncos passes through, chirping around the dooryard and making the crumbs I throw to them disappear like magic. They are cheerful and chubby and I like to see their little black heads bob up and down and their spaded tails flirt gaily. Then three robins come, including, I am sure, my original two. For two solid hours they sit on a big cedar stump and in a wild cherry tree close by, looking everything over with thoroughness and disgust, for the snowy ground is still hard with the night's frost and nesting prospects are far from alluring. The feeding station is filled with food and a new robin house is painted and in place, but I am far from hopeful. Hyacinth, crocus, iris and tulip are pushing their way through the earth, and the buds on bush and tree are swelling with life — but what will spring be if there are no birds to set it to music?

But the birds come — and many of them stay. Each morning

the chirrup of the robin, the silver-threaded song of the winter wren and the clear bell notes of the varied thrush or Alaska robin envelop the cabin in melody. Purple finch, golden-crowned sparrow and white-breasted nuthatch share my breakfast before twittering off over the newly dug vegetable plots, and a yellow-headed blackbird is a two-day visitor. Near Dubh Glas, that dark pool of Teal River, Lord and Lady Harlequin Duck pose graciously on two stones near the bank, while in the pool itself a Barrow's goldeneye swims and dives in bachelor independence, his courting ritual of bobs and flourishes not yet begun. The two buffleheads, which have gone up the Wren as usual, will soon come down again, complete with family.

The earth is born again each year, and so are we. I know it when the first warm, bracken-scented wind creeps down from the uplands, and the sun slowly descends the mountains to spread its golden length along the winter-darkened valley. I know it when the moss — which faded to such pale green under the bleaching snows of winter — begins to take on its rich velvet darkness again and to raise itself from the softening earth; when the new twigs of the huckleberry glow as though red wine were running in their veins and the elderberry buds flush pink through the hard green of their fullness; when the blackberry shoots show an amethyst tinge, while the Hooker and long-leaved willows display orange-red and red-brown stems beside the rushing white waters of the rivers. The black willow accompanies the roaring streams down from the hills, and its soft gray pods — softer than any pussy I have known — have the gentle gleam of old pewter against the heavy darkness of the conifers. Low plants of forest and clearing show a crisp green over the brown of old grasses and the decay of fallen trees.

Around my special friend, the Douglas fir, the heart-shaped leaves of the yellow violet cover the snow-drenched earth, and trillium buds show whiteness beside the forest paths. In early morning and again at twilight the birds pour out their hearts from the edge of the woodland. Savannah and white-crowned sparrow share the grass seed amiably and the celestial mountain bluebird is seen in passage. Downy woodpecker, stellar jay, red-naped sapsucker, black-headed grosbeak and belted kingfisher flash across my clearing, and the song of the water ouzel rises even more clearly and sweetly than before. Chipmunks shrill from the stumps and the geese have gone over.

Down in the village they are a good two weeks ahead of me. The gardens are glowing with color and all the trees and bushes are shyly showing their infant leaves. But, to me, the reluctance of this mountain spring makes it all the lovelier. There is no rush of plenty to dull the senses, but as each new beauty appears there is time to appreciate and ponder it. At night the moon sails a clear sky, and by morning there is a thin icing of frost over everything to accentuate the golden warmth of later day. I never know what that day will bring:

> . . . *Daffodils,*
> *That come before the swallow dares and take*
> *The winds of March with beauty. . . .*

the arrival of a new bird acquaintance or an old feathered friend, a swarm of Compton tortoiseshell butterflies like sunlight on the path or the dark loveliness of a mourning cloak floating silently past me. Swift beauty, slow beauty to fill my heart. For,

> *Whan that Apprille with his shoures sote*
> *The droghte of Marche hath perced to the rote . . .*

time goes from sun to shower with elfin speed. During the days of warmth the wild pink currant breaks into lovely bloom and the American tortoiseshell and blue butterflies flit colorfully through the garden. The tent caterpillar moth is there also, and toward evening the polyphemus, the twin-spotted hawk, the lilac sphinx, the dark wood nymph and the exquisite saltmarsh tiger moth show themselves on the veranda or near my lamp. Black, green, long-horned and scarab beetles run busily around and when I am weeding a rock garden, some small brown relative bites my hand severely. During the sunny intervals of these days fires are started, for all burning must be done by the first of May and when the sun disappears in the late afternoon, it is like fall again with the tang of wood smoke on the gray, chill air.

The flats are being hardened off outdoors and the cold frame is green with perennial shoots. It is possible to transplant parsley, lettuce, cabbage and onions and to move the caraway plants in the herb garden. Potatoes and peas are planted in due crop rotation, and the seeds of borage, dill, sweet basil, sorrel, lavender, sweet marjoram, broccoli, kohlrabi, turnip, brussels sprouts, sugar beet, carrot, endive, red beet, tendergreen and swiss chard go in day by day. Purple, yellow and white crocus flower in every garden bed while hyacinth, scilla and heuchera are in full bloom with the lenten roses fading beside them. But the ground is still cold, so the beans — bush and the flaming scarlet runner for the cabin walls — must wait, although I know it will not be long before the days are so full of warmth and sunshine that I shall be wishing for rain to do my watering for me.

For, with May, I am caught up in the full tide of spring. Narcissus, tulip and iris burst into flower, while rock plants are great splashes of yellow, rose and startling white against the grayness of their background. Huge blue and yellow pansies challenge the wild and golden dandelions from the prim security of their beds. The lovely whistling melody of the hermit thrush mingles with the clear five notes and metallic zings of the Calaveras and MacGillivray's warblers. In the deep forest the lilting, liquid song of the varied thrush sounds mysteriously and the red-shafted flicker cries exultantly as he darts from tree to tree. The rivers are Wagner during the dark hours, but by day they are green and white adventurers storming through the mountain passes to carry their colors to the sea. The nights are still cool and clear, but the sun is passionate and demanding. The pale green leaves of bush and deciduous tree grow feverishly and the shepherd crooks of the bracken fern uncurl almost with a snap.

So, early one fragrant morning,

For May wol have no slogardye a-night.
The sesoun priketh every gentil herte,
And maketh him out of his sleep to sterte.

May and I go walking along Home Wood Trail. It is an old trail, used by Indians and explorers and by the prospectors who came to this particular part of the country over a hundred years ago. Until fairly recently it was a navigable wagon road running down to the village, but for ten years or so before I came it had been neglected and disused, and now a long stretch in the middle has been washed away by spring and autumn floods. So the trail ends sharply in a flare of steep rock running up the lower end of Silver Pine where that mountain curves down to meet the Teal some four miles from my door. It begins in my backyard, and my land is the connecting link between it and Mountain Trail, which runs eastward along Cougar mountain on the east side of the Wren and the south side of the Teal.

A week of very warm weather has brought bush and flower almost to full leaf, but they have not yet begun to sprawl across the path and so walking is as easy now as in April — and much less damp! A brilliant rufous hummingbird zings through the salmonberry brush at the beginning of the trail and a white admiral butterfly drifts gently by. A mountain chickadee peers at me from a branch, while from the Teal the wild, sharp cry of the kingfisher comes on the light breeze that is just stirring the tops of the tall evergreens. Nearby a squirrel scolds me fervently, and some distance away I can hear a woodpecker industriously at work. My old fir companion, to the left of this trail just as it enters the forest, stands now in a great pool of violets fringed with the green of forest plants not yet blooming. The shining leaves of twinflower and the soft green of moss cover rocks and ground — with great patches of alpine beauty, dwarf cornel and western trillium blazing white between them. The trail has been running straight west, but now it turns sharply north toward the Teal, with a great rockery rising up to the left in a miracle of green,

Annihilating all that's made
To a green thought in a green shade.

Moss covers every stone of it with sword (called "Christmas" in my mountains) shield and maidenhair fern growing between in exactly the right places. My own rockeries seem puny and gross in comparison, and I never see this perfect one of nature's without wishing that I could carry it home with me.

Now the trail plunges down a steep, short hill to run along the cliff side for a hundred yards or so. Shy, mauve-pink calypsos bloom beside it and the heavenly starflowers lend it their light. Beyond, where the path turns northwest and inland, the violets come again — in such numbers that it is almost impossible to keep from trampling them. The path is a green aisle stretching farther and farther back through hemlock, fir and cedar with the shouting of the Teal coming only faintly now across stunted yew and thimbleberry brush. In clearings here and there the sun pours warmly down upon the delicate rose flowers of the vine maple and the feathery goatsbeard. Great holes indicate where prospectors have been tracking gold, and the death sign of the logger is seen in the severed trunks lying where they have fallen because they could not be used for poles or in the sawmill, which operated near the railroad until twelve years ago. I have been told that there is an ordinance requiring all timber leavings to be cleared away, but if so it has never been obeyed here. Branches, tops and whole trunks make walking a series of hurdles, and worst of all the fire menace increases yearly. I do what I can, but even without the loggers I would be kept busy, for the great winds of winter and of March leave no path unchanged.

A mile farther, a side way lunges to the north toward the river, but my trail goes up a little hill to where a grove of red and blue huckleberry bushes stretches back among the conifers. In July and August it is like coming through a Christmas wood decked out in blue and scarlet, but now there is only the green leaf which so resembles that of the wild rose growing beside it. Beyond is a strange and lovely place with cedar, yew and vine maple twisted into fantastic shapes, and the ground glows with bleeding-heart and fairy bells. The path swings steadily in the direction of the river now and the voice of the spring waters becomes louder and deeper. Then it is shouting in my ears and I am standing on the banks of the Teal with Cedar Shake cabin at my back and the white beauty of two wild cherry trees above my head.

The lovely salmonberry blossoms blush beside me, with prince's pine and false solomon's seal adding their delicate pink and white touches here and there. The wild blackberry is not yet blooming, but nearby patches of low Oregon grape and wild ginger show green-yellow flowers — if you are enterprising enough to search for them — with the prickly devil's club spreading its gigantic foliage over them like a parasol. The wild pink currant glows against walls of cedar shakes and against the green of the waters going so powerfully by. This cabin, built by prospectors and now abandoned, is on one border of my property. Surely no one's land was ever bounded by greater loveliness.

After this the river is left a little way behind and there is much balancing on logs and thin planks over deep gullies sunlit with violets. Then down to the Teal once again — flowing in shallow green and amber — and across a sandy beach where red columbine has found a foothold and baneberry waves a plumed white head. Musk (but with no musky scent) and yellow arum — that lovely flower with the unlovely odor when it is crushed or wilting — bloom in the woods behind, where the old trail ran before the pole cutters went through. Now, instead of following precipitately along the sides of Silver Pine where the flowers of the wild strawberry are white drifts below the evergreens, the path goes through the bottomlands for perhaps half a mile, only striking up the steep slope just before a small stream comes plunging down from the heights above. Up there this stream is a waterfall of ivory spray, but when it careens across Home Wood Trail it has become four swift brooks, not one of which it is possible to cross dry-shod.

On either side and rising to the very top of Silver Pine is a gigantic rock garden done in deep emerald and delicate pastels. Moss-covered boulders lie under and around the crystal water, and each miniature creek has the pink, white or yellow flowers of snowberry, creeping raspberry and bush honeysuckle showing somewhere along its banks. The maidenhair fern is luxuriant here, adding its green feathery coolness to the dancing water.

Everything is so new and clean on this trail and at this time. It is indeed as though the world's eternal day had come and there would never be another night. The young hemlocks seem scrubbed to paleness and the firs have a gloss to them that comes at no other season. Even the old cedars have shaken off the dust of years and when the sun shines through them, a faint, silvery radiance gleams from their dark branches. Life is everywhere, surging through petal, wing and limb. Nothing is still, nothing completely silent. The sun flashes from the racing waters of the river; white clouds move across a deep blue sky; a flock of Vaux's swifts mounts in graceful, curving flight; and over and above it all rise the wild, sweet songs of mating time.

Masses of Oregon grape with shining, evergreen luster on holly-like leaves follow my footsteps as I walk — gradually southward and away from the Teal — toward the House of the Seven Dwarfs. This is a log cabin, also built by prospectors, that stands back in the deep woods with only the white flowers of spring to brighten it. It is in good repair, but I notice that a falling hemlock has neatly sheared the front porch below the high, peaked roof — like that of the old fairy tale — and I think of how storms must seem in this dim place, with the tall trees standing close and the bush crowding by. They would be like the sea breaking in violence overhead, with now and then a loud, sharp report as a branch breaks off or a fir top is severed. At intervals would come the cr-r-rack of falling timber and then a great tearing, crashing sound as a tree plunged down to lie across moss and underbrush. There would be ghostly voices from the river at night, and by day only a little sunlight would be able to penetrate the closely growing conifers. A strange situation for a house, surely, but when one has an eye on gold perhaps everything else becomes invisible.

"The Diggins" lies just beyond, where piles of rock and gravel show the patient and impatient work of those who sought colors in metal rather than, as I do, in sunlight and flower and shining sand. Western dogwood and the bog cranberry lighten the harsh, gray channel with their creamy bloom, while the small white flowers of the black cap show at intervals. But their berries seldom ripen, for they need more sun than they can find here. The river is only a faint sound now, but a sudden rattling breaks the silence and I look up to see a Lewis's woodpecker darting from tree to tree to excavate violently — perhaps the prospectors have spurred him on — or just to cling there and look down at me with sharp, bright eyes.

This curving channel, running to the Teal at both ends, has made an island of the territory lying between it and the river. This has been stringently logged over, but it is lovely still and as I cross it I hear the waters beyond speaking loudly and clearly with the voice of spring. Where my path joins the Teal there are willowwashes with violets yellow beside them and rosy fringecup spangling the green of moss and shining pipsissewa leaves. Hemlock, yew and cottonwood stand sparsely, and tiny waterfalls drop from high cliffs to my left, which are covered with ferns and creeping plants. A tall gooseberry bush flaunts its white blossoms beside a California hazelnut and as I turn sharply west along the Teal, I find the ivory flowers of the red elderberry growing beside my path.

Then, suddenly, I am at the end, with a tiny meadow of bleeding-heart to my left and the sheer side of Silver Pine before me. Two spotted sandpipers teeter along a stretch of beach and, on a pile of driftwood across the river, I catch a glimpse of two spring visitors, Mr. and Mrs. Golden Plover. Just behind them, on the north bank of the Teal, is Timber Trail and a group of loggers' cabins. Fireweed mountain looms above them with the raucous cry of a jay ringing down from its flowered slopes. A western flycatcher flashes up the river like sunlight, and an osprey circles slowly overhead. If I could only paint this beauty and this peace — or write it down or pattern it into a melody of May! But I have no way — no way at all — in which to tell you. It is all in my heart, but when I try to place on paper the sound of spring water flowing, the birdsongs and the fragrant wind whispering through leaf and blossom, nothing appears but strange, misshapen words that bear only a travesty of resemblance to all this loveliness.

Is May really a more charming month than any other, or do I just think so because it is May now and I am walking home through the cool, scented forest after a morning of happiness with spring? Probably the latter, for to each month I swear that I love it above all the others — and when I say that, I do not feel I lie. But spring — delicate, dancing spring of the pale gold hair and the green eyes! Clear, sweet air and rushing water; perfume of hyacinth and newly spaded earth; the first bird and bud and butterfly — and my own first hour again.

The dawns of May are silver chilled by night and by the snows that still lie deep on the high mountains. They come delicately to my door and lay cool fingers on my face when I step out into the first light of morning. Trill and warble, whistle and chirp come from all around, and the sun flows down the dark sides of Evergreen and Fireweed to fill my valley with brightness and warmth again. The days are golden, not the yellow gold of summer, but a green-gold thin and newly shining. Dusk comes softly and goes reluctantly. Moths flutter silently here and there, a bee falls fast asleep in a yellow iris and birdsongs dwindle and fade into sleepy twitterings. A May moon glimmers in the darkening sky and the scent of narcissus and early lily drifts across the face of night. My valley and I fall asleep in spring and awaken to find the rose of June unfolding.

3

Sun
in the valley

Inebriate of air am I,
And debauchee of dew,
Reeling, through endless summer days,
From inns of molten blue.

EMILY DICKINSON

The host of summer has come to sit at table with his numberless guests. Sap, juice and honey are his beverages and every fruit, vegetable and herb is piled high on the earthen platters. In June the feasting begins and the leaves fly before it is ended.

June — that is a month for you! Dawns like dream extended into waking; long days of warmth and color, with nights more delicately scented than any lady of the heart. It is always too early to go to bed, and daylight seems far too late a time at which to rise. There is so much to see, so much to do. The first annual blossoms, the first vegetable is eaten. The rivers recede and soon are only a background of murmuring. The grass has its first cutting and the first salmonberry, red and juicy, is discovered. Two speckled blue eggs in a corner of the side veranda turn into gaping beaks, and a baby wren, the size of a semicolon, falls from its nest under a stump near its namesake river. Also, my Roman bathing begins.

The best size for a bathroom is as big as all outdoors. Sky-blue ceiling, evergreen walls, sanded brown floor and superbly air-conditioned — the bathroom I have betters all the plans of all the architects for the streamlined houses of an atomic world. If I wish, I can use a new tub each morning, and there are no heating restrictions. Lying in one of the many pools left between the boulders by the receding river with hot stones underneath me and the water a foot deep, I can fairly simmer. For a bracing rinse afterward there are the cool, green depths of that big pool, Dubh Glas.

Two hours of weeding and spraying made an excellent appetizer for a bath, especially when heightened by the thought that "there is no ancient gentlemen but gardeners . . . they hold up Adam's profession." The sun is just above the mountains then and the cabin, when I go back to it for soap and towel, is dark and cool. Robin, warbler and thrush are making morning music while a calliope hummingbird is vibrating over a patch of sunlit clarkia. Bee flies and butterflies are warming themselves, and an ant lion, belying his name, goes delicately by. Halfway down the path to the Teal a shaft of sunlight strikes across late-blooming blue and yellow iris and the budding sweet william beside them. It lights up the many small beds and rock gardens in this part of the grounds and floods the stumps that brim with pansy, alyssum and dwarf wallflower.

The vegetable gardens and strawberry beds — "Doubtless God could have made a better berry, but doubtless God never did" — are in full sun and so is the large flowerbed on the knoll where jasmine, heuchera, phlox and matricaria live amicably together. Then past the dewy gold and flame of Mrs. Dupont and Paul Scarlet, the colorful disorder of the wildflower bed and down the stone steps that divide the big rock garden fronting the Teal. To the left, on the flat below, beans, peas, potatoes and sugar beets show blossom, leaf and pod. To the right, on a small island that has the Wren on one side and a dry — except in early spring and late fall — watercourse on the other, my water tank and tower stand almost hidden among the trees. Chamomile — which I like to call mayweed — spreads a white carpet at the base, with woolly sunflower and purple fleabane weaving through it, like Assyrian cohorts in purple and gold.

Near the Teal cage platform an inchworm humps himself along a bush honeysuckle which is already displaying its Ethiopian twins in their crimson cradles. A squash bug (my neighbors delight in calling it "stink bug"!) explores a young broadleaf maple and a sexton beetle goes funereally by. I remember that exciting time when I watched one bury a young robin. I had been here two years before I actually saw an interment, although I had come across several carcasses with larvae on them or with plump young grubs feeding.

Just below the platform the gravel begins, with the pink of bird's-foot clover and the blue of self-heal springing hardily out of it. These plants seem to live — and thrive — on air. Self-heal (or heal-all) — used for quinsy and sores by early settlers — looks fairly rugged, but the clover is as delicate as a hummingbird's claw and seems so fragile that its environment is a constant wonder to me. Both transplant easily, but the difficulty is that they want my rock garden entirely to themselves and do some very rude jostling! Varicolored stones glimmer around the flowers in green and white and rose where the spring floods have left them. Slate, granite, serpentine, chert and quartz are found here with many others — some of which make interesting book ends or impressive doorstops and paperweights. Thinking of the times I have shopped in crowds and heat and rush for such articles, I feel that not to have to do so any more is one of the most delightful things about this wilderness life of mine. Now I can take a leisurely stroll into the woods in February to pick up the small, perfect cones that fall from the hemlocks to lie darkly on the snow. In autumn and early winter I can look for the larger cones of pine and fir with which to make table or Christmas decorations or come home with tough yew and sweet-smelling cedar for various useful and ornamental bits of carpentry. After one has lived here for a time it is impossible to walk anywhere unobservantly. The ear is always alert to song, rustle or padding tread; the eye checks flower, tree and path, with a special regard to fire and workshop wood; the nose positively weaves from side to side endeavoring to identify whiffs of blossom, bark and hide. Even the tongue shares in these excursions, with nibble of gum or needle mingling with the primeval taste of earth and water that is always on it.

This June sun is too warm and golden for anything but a slow saunter over the stones, picking one up here and there to add to my garden markers. (To lessen the danger of a careless night foot — my own, for instance — I border those plots adjoining a path with quartz and porphyry, keeping the darker bits for more distant beds.) I stop to explore the fresh piles of driftwood left by high water. Some good pieces may be in there for burning when they are well dried, but seasoned driftwood — because of the gravel in it — is hard on ax and saw and temper. This debris of the flood is piled on the east end of one of my islands. I have two (thereby doubling a great childish ambition): one in each river and they have both increased in area by many feet since I came here. I have no objection to acquiring more real estate, but — every good thing bringing its reverse with it — this has so narrowed the Teal that now I have to go almost a quarter of a mile to wade it, even at its lowest.

I sit down on one of the logs, and the sun is like a great yellow Persian cat stretched beside me, with the river purring contentedly for us both. Now I can look up and down the Teal, but not very far because of the many bends in it. I can see the mountains of the Endahwin Range, with snow still on their peaks, to the

west (many miles beyond the end of Home Wood Trail) and those of the Cocoosh Range to the east and southeast with Cougar mountain in front of them just across the Wren. Evergreen is at my back; Fireweed faces me beyond the Teal and the forest through which run Timber Trail and Swamp Road. "In rivers, the water that you touch is the last of what has passed and the first of that which comes: so with time present," and I know that when I look up and down the Teal I am viewing not only east and west, but also past and future in this quiet "now." This scene before me is the direct antithesis of so much that has gone on in the outside world for so many years and of the perverted thinking that has brought it about. Here are serenity, security and beauty, with creation, not destruction coming out of every seed that is dropped by bird or wind or that is sown by my hand.

On every continent, in war and in peace, the tendency has been to encourage twisted thought. One could almost believe that there was a gigantic conspiracy to bring about those very horrors which later we decry with uplifted hands and eyes. Newspapers, magazines, radio and television — all those instruments that should be striving to lift public opinion toward a great crescendo of truth and beauty — play over and over again those coarse dissonances that vibrate only in the lowest instincts of humanity. I sometimes wonder if those who support the theory that if the public is foolish enough to pay for dirt, then dirt they shall have, ever see a connection between their attitude and the loss and maiming of their children by war, disease or poverty? One does not have to be poor oneself to die from the effects of want.

To die: that is the verb which conjugates the world. It is the only tenet of our faith in which we truly believe. We are still crusaders slaughtering, physically or mentally, those whom we consider to be heathen in order that the stream of their blood may sweep us into heaven. To die - to kill - to die! Never to live, to affirm vitality, to believe that happiness and not sorrow is our birthright. By what curious twist of thought do we arrive at the conclusion that there is nothing good in this world and that all light and well-being exist only in a problematical world to come? The evil there is in this world we have put into it ourselves, and we are as able to drain those dark sewers as we were to fill them. Nothing but ourselves prevents us from pouring into them those living waters of truth, kindness, beauty and happiness; to grow heaven here and now upon this waiting plot of earth.

It has taken me nearly all my life so far to find out that this is life for me. Looking back, those years are like time spent wandering in the wilderness. How strange that must seem to those who think that I am in the wilderness now! Some years of my childhood were not altogether wasted, but except for isolated periods here and there I cannot think of any others that may be listed on the asset side of my personal ledger. Most of the rest were spent in cities, surrounded by all the luxuries and leisure-making gadgets of so-called civilization. But they failed to make any leisure — only time to be thrown away or "killed." I was a killer then, certainly; I had no acquaintance with happiness or content, but only with brittle pleasure which cut my grasping hand. I surrounded myself with acquaintances who needed only the wind of my going into a different life than theirs to blow them away from me. I catered to the opinions of my neighbors as to how I should act or even think and went about in a moribund condition because I was sure that if I began to live my own life the gossip tongues would shred my thin skin to ribbons.

But my hide was tougher than I thought. Certain ties had to be broken, but they should have been severed long before. That was the one thing I had dreaded most: that I would hurt someone. That is also the one thing — as I can see now, but could not see then — that has played more havoc with my life than any other. Actually, no one was hurt; although a few thought they were. They were only impatient, scornful, critical and angry. When we are completely true to ourselves, things usually work out for us, but even if they do not it is still better to be true. To persist in a mistake may, perhaps, take away the ultimate happiness of others besides ourselves, and we have no right to play God.

I think that kindness and courage are the two attributes that we human beings need most. The courage to hear the truth without rancor or excuse; the courage and kindness to speak it without apology or smugness. There is really no need for man to be the lonely being he is. It is fear and pretense that have forced him into that state and kept him there. It is we ourselves who have thrown up the walls that divide us from each other and against which we beat desperate, impotent hands.

> *"Prisoner, tell me, who was it who wrought this unbreakable chain?"*
> *"It was I," said the prisoner, "who forged this chain very carefully."*

The black moments of loneliness come and we cry: "I cannot bear this any longer! I *must* speak!" But to whom — and how? Either we cannot show ourselves clearly or, if we can, we have delivered a weapon into the hands of our enemy, the friend. Then the black moments become darker than any stygian night, and despair is a great emptiness filling us with nothing. Kindness and courage, they could remake the world.

It is startling to find that the sun must be over half an hour higher than when I sat down on this driftwood. A bath tub — quickly! Here is a splendid one, almost encircled by boulders. The water is over a foot deep and warmer than the Gulf of Mexico. The stones at the bottom are smooth and rounded and I can lie full-length with ease. Ah, this is heaven! I prop my head on a rock and stretch out, covered with water to my chin, looking up into the clear face of the summer sky. A dipper goes into his song and dance on a rock nearby, and a kingfisher, from his gallery seat on the cage cable, gives a Bronx cheer. A mourning cloak butterfly alights beside me, dark against the dazzling white of limestone, and makes rhythm with its wings. The sun strikes full on rocks and river and the reflection hurts my eyes. I close them and relax in the warmth of the water, with Chaucer's words running through my mind:

> *Now welcom, somer, with thy sonne softe,*
> *That hast this wintres weders overshake.*

But other words are there also — and not such pleasant ones. My brain refuses to stop grinding out thoughts today, very much like sausage, probably, for there are so many ingredients and they are so thoroughly mixed. About hurting people: I wonder if I have, perhaps, been self-deceived all this time and

was merely afraid of being hurt myself. I had been, too, but we should never allow ourselves to be disturbed by such trivialities. Each one of us has a life to live. It is our own life and no one can live it for us. Very, very few people in this world ever manage to live a life. The ones who do are always criticized, if nothing worse, but they are the only truly happy human beings. Those who try to live but do not quite succeed are the unhappy ones. The world sees to that, even though it may tender posthumous recognition of that which they were trying to do. Over two thousand years ago Mimnermus said: "We are all clever enough at envying a famous man while he is yet alive, and at praising him when he is dead." How little difference two thousand years can make!

Actually, I am going toward life instead of trying to escape from it. I am searching for the very source of being in all its manifestations. Back in the city everything is covered with so many layers of artificiality, deceit and wishful thinking that it is impossible to know where truth begins and pretense ends. There is so little of vigor and vitality, locked away as a town is from the fecund soil by asphalt and by steel. But here I am renewed each morning, and each night I know that I have gone a little further toward serenity, strength and self-knowledge.

> *To know that all is well, even if late*
> *We come to know it, is at least some gain.*

I have left nothing behind that cannot be done better by others; I have brought with me the one thing in which I am, perhaps, a little more skilled than the average. I can work harder here than there, and the results are better. "I have no superfluous leisure," but yet am not one of those of whom it has been said: "These, too, are triflers who have wearied themselves in life by their activity." I know that I am, to the limit of my ability, contributing to humanity. To the community also, for my other small talent, making things grow, has helped many larders. "I am a true laborer: I earn that I eat, get that I wear, owe no man hate, envy no man's happiness, glad of other men's good."

But what was that about larders? Food! It must be nearly eight and there is still the fire to light, the salmonberries to pick, the cereal to cook. I soap, rinse, dry and dress myself hastily. A willow thrush inspects me carefully and then goes teetering madly away as I turn toward the steps. A red-naped sapsucker darts to a hemlock on the bank, and a flock of common goldfinch (called "wild canaries" here) flutters down and as quickly flutters up again. As I hurry across the lower flat, trailing blackberry vines — flowering in white beauty — clutch at my ankles, and black cap bushes try to detain me. The fruit of my saskatoons is almost ripe and all the untilled ground is fragrant and rosy with sweet wild strawberries.

I feel utterly refreshed. I have been free in mind and body as I bathed. How pitiful the confining bathroom, the crowded resort beaches of lake and ocean! For others, but not for me. There will be many to praise them, but here there is only I to tell of the beauty and peace that are all around me; of the waters — surely those eternal waters — that are the source and meaning of my life.

4

The pilgrimage

And smale fowles maken melodye,
That slepen al the night with open yë
(So priketh hem nature in hir corages);
Thanne longen folk to goon on pilgrimages.

CHAUCER

I do not need the red squirrels sliding down my roof, the robins uttering plump chirps on the lawn or a hermit thrush whistling by my woodshed to wake me on a June morning. When the heights of Evergreen are still dark outside my window and the earth is silent in sleep, I am out in the vegetable patch hoeing, weeding and transplanting. This is one of the loveliest times of day. The air is cool and fragrant and that holy feeling of communion with the soil fills me completely. Such an exultancy wells up in me as I walk among my growing things! It is second — and by only a small margin — to that terrible joy I feel in the creation of a piece of writing. Here, in my gardens, I have not given birth myself but have only assisted in the delivery room. Yet the two experiences are so closely bound that it seems that one could not have come into existence without the other.

I put more stakes in for the tomatoes and see that the peavines are bearing up under their load. There will be lettuce, radishes, onions and small raw carrots for lunch, with swiss chard and potatoes for dinner. Turnip and beet tops provide variety, while soon the pea pods will be bursting with fullness and the bush beans will be long and tender as well as green. Achillea, scarlet phlox and polemonium make the borders of my useful plots patriotic and ornamental. The flower pot stumps sing clearly in red, white, blue and yellow, and the beds are filled with the blossoms of spring and early summer together with the buds of July. The pocket-handkerchief lawn is green and soft, with red and yellow salmonberries hanging deliciously over it. My heart is so happy that surely it also must burst into flower!

Very early on these mornings the light comes "forth with pilgrim steps, in amice gray," and even the highest trees on the mountain are still in shadow. Then rosy little clouds come drifting over Evergreen, and the sun begins to creep down the tall trunks, lower and lower until it strikes the topmost branches of Home Wood and slides goldenly to the mossy ground. The cabin and its garden are still in shade, but the river is sparkling with sun. Bushes are dew spangled and the fresh, earthy smell is like the very scent of heaven. Why do we build cathedrals of brick and stone when there are hills, woods and rivers where we can worship so much more simply and beautifully? How far we have come from that divine simplicity taught by Christ! He went away from cities into the solitude of the mountains and he preached beside the sea. To us a tree is so much timber, a river so much power and a hill — well, in a hill there may be gold.

When I was a child, I lay on the summer grass looking up at the big, white clouds and imagining that they were the towers and turrets of heaven. How simple everything was in those days! Now, for me, it is simple once again, after long years of needless complication. I know this: there has been thanksgiving in my heart every hour of every day since I came to this place. Here I have found faith, courage, truth and such beauty that even if there is no heaven after all, in the clouds or above them, yet I shall have walked its paths and sat beside its streams.

Now the sun is stretching long fingers across the knoll to touch my writing chair and table there — both built from old chopping blocks and painted green — and I know that I must bathe, breakfast and do house and woodshed chores, which are no chores really, but merely part of the great pleasure of living in this place — or of just living. Mr. and Mrs. Robin are listening for worms nearby and the dawn chorus is in full voice when I turn to go back to the cabin. Scales, arpeggios and trills cascade down from the trees as warbler, thrush, wren, Say's phoebe and blackheaded grosbeak pour out silver melody to flow upon gold-

en sunlight. The robins join them and then, shrill with envy, jay, woodpecker and kingfisher go shrieking across the clearing. In the pauses the crystal notes of the water ouzel rise up from the river accompanied by the wren's own liquid, rushing song. Bees stir sleepily in blossoms and hummingbirds hover above the window boxes. It will be difficult to leave all this, even for a little pilgrimage to my neighbor's.

My neighbor is Bill, an old prospector with "a certain jollity of mind pickled in the scorn of fortune," who has roamed these mountains or others like them for over seventy years. Some of his tales are taller than he — and he is well over six feet still, only a little bowed by years and many packboard loads — but all of them are told with such dry humor and with such twinkling of blue eyes in a brown parchment face, that they are irresistible. Bill, praise be, will always "want that glib and oily art, to speak and purpose not." He knows that his stories are stretched to snapping point — and he knows that I know it. This is half the fun of the whole thing, but his herbal lore is sound. I can testify to that after using the young shoots of yellow arum as a spring tonic, the grated root stalks of false solomon's seal (wild onion does just as well) as a poultice and Oregon grape roots for a stomach upset.

Pansy, arabis, iberis, alyssum, armeria, aubrietia, helian-themum, lobelia, gentian,

> God made a little gentian;
> It tried to be a rose
> And failed, and all the summer laughed.

ice plant, tunica and verbena are jeweling the rock gardens, and my wildflower plot is blooming joyfully as I go down to the Teal with my lunch and a few gifts for Bill in my knapsack. The water is still high — too high for wading — so I swing out on the cage with a breeze of my own making in my face and the roar of the river below me. I doubt if any visitor will ever forget that cage, especially the ones who arrive by train in the middle of the night and have to walk miles along the railroad track and then across and down a mountain by bush trails. At the end of that arduous journey they find a homemade ladder rising fifteen feet up into the air with a frail platform on top where the cage swings on a thick wire rope attached to a big hemlock.

The ladder wobbles a bit and the platform distinctly moves, while the river roars below with what might pass anywhere for savagery. There is only one small lantern to push back the dark-ness, and it seems that we are going to launch ourselves into a black void on three unsubstantial boards. My guest climbs on, I unfasten the hook and follow and then we are rushing through the night as though we were riding the wind. In a moment the sound of the river is behind us and we are pulling over small willows up to the home landing with our lantern swinging from the prow. That trip is something to be remembered, especially when the rivers are in flood and there seems to be no sound in all the world but that of thundering water.

But by daylight it is a bright, familiar thing and I find it very pleasant this June morning to idle slowly across, stopping every now and then to look up and down the Teal. It is the same scene, yet never the same. Now coral honeysuckle flashes its bright trumpets from between the huge leaves of broadleaf maple on the opposite shore, a sharp-shinned hawk drifts lazily overhead and from somewhere hidden comes the spiraling song of the olive-backed thrush. That sound reminds me of Maestro. Maestro is a Sierra hermit thrush who sings outside my bedroom window each dawn and dusk from May until September. Yes, even in September he essays a few pathetic notes, a stammering travesty of his full, rich song of summer. There are a great many hermit thrushes nesting near by cabin, but Maestro is the most glorious singer of them all. One of his relatives sounds like a rummage sale, he is always in such a hurry to finish; another is off key; still another gives the effect of having a wee bottle under his wing.

But with Maestro each note is rounded, each song complete. He is an artist. He is also, I believe, somewhat of an albino for his thrush markings are barely visible, and his chest is a much paler gray than that of the usual Sierra hermit. When his throat puffs out with singing, it is almost white. But his eye is a roving dark one, and he is very plump and trim in his brown morning coat, which seems to have become a bit green as to back and slightly rusty as to tail — from wear, no doubt. We have long conversations together, although I believe he is almost ready to give me up as a singing pupil. I am no credit to him, certainly, and when he hides "his head under his wing,/Poor thing," he probably has horrible dreams of my roving the woods, emitting those ear-revolting discords that I think are his beautiful song. But I *have* mastered his call note and now he gives it night and morning — and occasionally through the day — until I answer. I have also acquired the "weet" with which he talks to himself and his cronies, but his "snore" — in broad daylight with his eyes wide open! — is beyond me.

One of Maestro's rackety relatives opens up as I walk away from the ladder northward toward Fireweed with alder, aspen, willow and cottonwood all around me and berry bushes brushing against my thighs. Fern and foamflowers mingle, rather aloofly, with the unsociable devil's club, while the delicate twinflower and miner's lettuce clamber over logs or picture themselves against the smooth green of moss. Now there are maples and young conifers and then an open, park-like space with hemlock, fir and cedar standing straight and tall within green space and quietness. The sunlight, slanting through the tree trunks on to mossy ground so beautifully clear of under-brush, has the color of tokay and the air, its full and fragrant sweetness. Water once came through here in spring and fall, so logs were laid down many years ago, which are welcome even now because of the swampiness of those seasons.

At the far side of this enclosure wrens are bustling about and a brown creeper is insect hunting. A red-eyed vireo — that not very solemn "preacher bird" — flings leisured melody across yellow avens and blue brookline. A great wild rosebush, nearly six feet tall, is the lovely signpost at the intersection of Main Street and Swamp Road. I have been following the former — so called because it is one of the main trails up over Fireweed mountain to the railroad, crossing Village Road on the way — but it is by the latter that I shall probably come home. Swamp Road and Timber Trail duplicate Mountain and Home Wood trails on the other side of the Teal, running, as they do, west to the village and east toward a tiny railroad community six miles beyond Bill's cabin. His house stands almost at the intersection of Swamp Road and Cougar Trail, which skirts the eastern end of Cougar mountain and runs through the high passes of the Cocoosh country, past Chert Lake and a hill town, to Gold Road.

Trappers, prospectors, travelers and settlers toiled along Cougar Trail and Gold Road in years gone by, and even now these are wide, open ways for the most part, easy to find and follow. Before the railroad came and a recent highway, which runs thirty miles south of Gold Road, they were the east-west, north-south arteries of this mountain land. But, used only by a few hunters and prospectors now, it will not be long before they are overgrown by brush and obstructed by windfalls, with sec-tions of them lost forever in one deep canyon or another.

After its meeting with Swamp Road, Main Street begins its climb, running through heavy timber for a mile or so to where it meets the broad Village Road. This wooded section is at its best in spring and early summer. I remember coming home late one night in early June with the soft light of my lantern falling on false Solomon's seal, twisted stalk, foamflower, a few alum root, starflower, alpine beauty, dwarf cornel, yellow violet, bleeding-heart, crimson salmonberry blossom, white thimbleberry and blackberry flower, the blushing wild currant, white trillium turning to crimson, Oregon grape, red columbine, pink twinflower, blue larkspur and the white bells of black nightshade — all in glorious bloom together. It was an unbelievable sensation to walk through such drifts and pools and hanging gardens of scent and color, flashing my light here and there to watch them come strangely and impressively out of the soft darkness. That was one night I said, with Faustus:

Stand still, you ever moving spheres of heaven,
That time may cease . . .

and also like him, for my soul's salvation.

Early June prefers the woodlands, but late June comes into its own on the open Village Road and the untimbered upper slopes of Fireweed. It was at this wide trail that the fire-fighters were able to stop the great flames that swept over the mountain a few years ago, leaving little but skeletons and ash behind. So now the slopes, as I walk east toward Bill's, have nothing living on them that is more than bush tall. But what bushes and what flowers between them! Fireweed shouts with color on this midsummer day and my heart shouts too, with joy that I am here to see it. Indian paintbrush, pink fleabane, yellow fennel (which once crowned victorious gladiators), Queen Anne's lace, white daisy, sagebrush, cow parsnip with its lacy leaves and wild clover — there seems to be no end to the hues and patterns woven through this glorious cloak thrown protectingly across devastated Fireweed. But it is not all shouting here; there are whispers also. Along the dry stream beds, which are such torrents in spring and fall, the delicate bluebell companions the elfin yellow monkey-flower which closes at a touch; maidenhair fern creeps from rock crevices to background blue beard-tongue and the white stars of field chickweed; the wild yellow lily nods to the tiny blue florets of speedwell, which the villagers call forget-me-not.

I want to run and sing as I go! I want to fling my arms wide to all this radiance and raise a paean to this golden hour! The sun shines down in noon warmth; the bridal perfume of syringa drifts intoxicatingly by; river, mountain and forest are spread out before me like a promise of heaven "framed in the prodigality of nature." I am drunk — I am quite delirious! It is too much for me or for any man.

The shade of a blue elderberry bush is just the right luncheon spot, as I munch raw vegetables and sourdough bread with cymes of white flowers waving over me and pert western buttercups peering up from below. "Lettuce," says Charles Dudley Warner in his sketch, *My Summer in a Garden*, "is like conversation: it must be fresh and crisp, so sparkling that you scarcely notice the bitter in it," but it is only the elderly who may become bitter. The tang of wild onion and the tonic breath of sage mingle, very suitably, with the flavor of my young, sweet leaves, while the fragrance of wild strawberry proclaims what my dessert will be. The taste of this small red berry is so much sweeter than that of the cultivated fruit, that sugar would be "coals to Newcastle." But it hides so skillfully under its low green leaves that picking becomes a treasure hunt and one devoutly wishes for "a cast-iron back, with a hinge in it."

There is one thing that distinguishes Village Road from most of the other trails I follow: it is the silence; "silence more musical than any song." On Timber, Mountain, Swamp and Home Wood trails and in my little cabin, the sound of running water is steady and insistent until, after a little while, it so weaves itself into the consciousness that you are not aware of its presence unless you wish to be. Yet it is always there. In summer and winter it is a sedate and quiet singing, but in autumn and spring it is a roistering mountain chorus. Yes, whatever I do has the sound of water running through it — until I climb Main Street and hear it grow fainter and fainter below, standing at last on Village Road in a core of silence. I feel suddenly deaf then, as though I were climbing to the peaks or losing altitude in an airplane, and it is several minutes before my ears can adjust themselves enough to distinguish those softer sounds usually hidden under the voices of my rivers. Then the drone of a bee becomes audible, the whirr of a dragonfly, the roll of a pebble, the faraway note of a tree toad and the swift slither of a striped garter snake through last year's leaves.

But the rivers can still be seen. They are gray threads running through green cloth one thousand feet below. Bone mountain, graveyard of another forest fire that is usually hidden behind Cougar, comes into view. A flock of yellow warblers (they share the name of a "wild canary" with the common goldfinch) flies down near a clump of false box, and some Brewer blackbirds go over in the direction of Bill's cherry trees.

These trees are a glorious sight in May — as are also, to a lesser degree, the wild cherry trees that grow near my cabin and on various trails — while down near the village the Oregon crabapple makes spring a delight. The dwarf bilberry grows near the village too and that is where the purple violets, those "deep, blue eyes of springtime," can be found in April with the glorious Pacific dogwood rising white above them. (Actually the flowers of this tree are green-yellow and small; it is the large white flower-bud scales that are so sensational and usually mistaken for the flower itself.) And right now, on this June day, the beautiful evergreen rhododendrons will be growing in the mountains high above the village; rosy banks of them in the dark passes where snow and wind go hurtling through in winter and where, even now, the ground is moist and cold. It is one of nature's many miracles that a conservatory bloom like this should flourish in such surroundings.

Where Cougar Trail crosses Village Road and lunges down the mountain toward Bill's, stonecrop, shrubby cinquefoil and wild mustard make a lovely farewell to the flowers of dry and sunny places before I return to those of the cool woods. I twist swiftly down with Cougar Trail, through shade and dappled light where salal grows and the melody of the song sparrow comes sweet and clear. Through a gap in the trees I can see Bill's bachelor cottage ("A cow is better than a woman; a woman uses too much wood") with its red roof, but there is no sign of the owner, so I sit down on a fir stump beside the shining leaves of silver-back and unship my binoculars for a bird hunt. Rough-winged swallows skim high above the cabin and the black caps of a flock of pileolated warblers bob up and down in the little orchard. I have discovered eight different families of the warbler clan in this district, but two of them — orange-crowned and Audubon's — are usually in the higher mountains during the summer. The black-throated gray, MacGillivray, Calaveras and Townsend chirp around my cabin until September, but for the others — pileolated and yellow — I have to come up here. The killdeer plover is not a rare sight down near the village, while on the higher slopes of Fireweed the ravens sometimes get together. Cooper's and the sharp-shinned hawk make life rather miserable for Bill's chickens, and flocks of purple finches occasionally do the same for his fruit trees. The less said the better of that astute robin family who built their nest on a cherry tree limb so that they might have breakfast in bed!

> *One of the ones that Midas touched,*
> *Who failed to touch us all,*
> *Was that confiding prodigal,*
> *The blissful oriole.*

That "fire bird" and "golden robin," Bullock's oriole, has proved here, by keeping down the insect pests in the orchard, that he can be useful as well as decorative. An old grandaddy of a pileolated woodpecker — called "cock o' the woods" — can be seen any day around this clearing, and the Say's phoebe turns up every now and then, while pipits and pine siskins make this a favorite way station in the fall.

- - - - - - - - - -

"Songs are sung and tales are told, darkness dreams upon the sky" when I set out for home. A full moon is rising over Sable mountain as I leave Bill's clearing and strike into the forest. My path follows a stream bed of ferns and mossy boulders precipitously down to the Teal and then swings directly west just along the bank, where the hungry river is nibbling at the trail. Beyond, the salmonberry brush is higher than my head and I have to find my way through it by the feel of the path under my feet. At the edge of the clearing where there are two old logging cabins, stinging nettles rake across my arm and I stand still, thinking for a moment that I can see the graceful dancers of the ballet *Swan Lake* move across the moonflooded clearing toward the glimmering water. The princess of that tale was not the only person who wove nettles into cloth; Europeans and Asiatics have made fine linen from them for centuries. The Indians here wove them into cord and the cord into fishing nets, besides using both roots and leaves as food. I can see tiny tents of the red admiral caterpillar on these leaves and if it were daylight, I am sure that I would find the green caterpillars of the tiger swallowtail on the nearby bitter cherry, embryo Compton tortoiseshell butterflies on the willows and most certainly the misleadingly named saltmarsh caterpillar of the dainty — and equally misnamed — saltmarsh tiger moth.

This night is too lovely to say goodnight in so, with the moonlight full on my face, I slip quietly past some deserted cabins and sit down on a log at the river's edge. As always, the hypnotism of its flowing is like a soft, compelling hand across my eyes and never more so than now when each ripple is enchanted to onyx or to silver, and darkness is a changeling of the moon.

A little way downstream I can see the shadow of the big cedar that was felled for a footbridge and now stretches from bank to bank. A young lad who was placer mining here a few years ago admitted to me that when he crossed it once at high water, he was so scared he "cooned" it along the tree trunk. I can imagine how the river snarled below him, reaching up with clammy, urgent fingers to loosen his grip of the narrow bridge. For the course of the Teal is direct and steep, so at all seasons of the year its voice can be heard — softly in midwinter and midsummer, loudly in fall and spring when the heavy rains and the freshets of melting snow turn it into a brown monster, raging from bank to bank and driving the driftwood before it. Bridges go out then and the growl of rolling boulders can be heard night and day.

The Teal has come seventeen miles to these cabins — from Teal Lake at an altitude of four thousand feet — and has twenty more to go before it merges with the big Mallard River and travels with it to the sea. There is not even a village on its way until it reaches the Mallard — only a few small, gray cabins huddled at intervals along the banks. Tributaries like the Wren flow into it here and there, coming down from the mountains of the Cocoosh and Endahwin Ranges. Accumulation of glacial debris has changed its course somewhat, but for the most part it follows the same channel as in pre-Pliocene times except that during the ages of its life it has cut down deeper and deeper between Fireweed and Cougar so that its bed now is a much narrower one than in, as the Indians say, "old time."

Where the Teal begins the snows lie deep in winter, and the handfuls of people who live at Teal Lake find the white ocean rising to their rooftops and have tunnels instead of paths connecting their houses. Fishermen from outside have almost emptied the lake of fish, but in the river and its tributaries — especially those like the Wren that are fairly inaccessible — rainbow and Dolly Varden trout dart and gleam and it is not difficult to get a good string at almost any time. In Dubh Glas, just outside my cabin, the big steelhead may be found — and caught on salmon eggs. "There is a river in Macedon, and there is also moreover a river at Monmouth . . . and there is salmons in both." On late afternoon of spring and summer I can see them jumping as dragon or damselflies flit over, but when I go after them with rod and line, they suddenly discover that the bouldered bottom of the pool is much more desirable than the exposed surface. That is when I know with Izaak Walton, that "angling will prove to be so pleasant that it will prove to be, like virtue, a reward in itself." Yet sometimes there are more material rewards also.

The night-scent of earth and the river-scent of water mingle in my nostrils as I walk slowly along my favorite part of Swamp Road: a clear, wide pathway carpeted with moss and leaves and roofed with evergreen and maple branches. Quietness lies here like deep velvet, with only the sound of cool water stirring it. No other large animal seems to be abroad tonight, but now and then a wood rat agitates the bracken. Moonlight filters through the trees, arabesques the forest floor and, where the trail contacts the river, makes pinpricks of argent light on ripple and tiny waterfall.

The way seems unbelievably short and almost before I know it, I am at the Main Street intersection once again. I never come out on the shores of the Teal just at this place without feeling a surge of joy at the sight of my little cabin snugged down between the mountains and the forest. It is so simple and real and lovely. Here is everything I want and more than I ever hoped to have. The green roof, the bark walls, the flowers, the vegetables, the filled woodshed — every tree, bush and stone, every foot of earth is dear to me. Inside, the words of friends fill my bookshelves, and my companion, fire, will come when I call him. There is no harsh speech, no lies, no bitterness anywhere; nothing but generosity, beauty and peace. I never knew before the real meaning of the word "home."

Now the cabin is just a dark outline silhouetted by the moon, but it is there and it is mine. Swiftly I climb the platform to the cage and launch myself out over the river. In a few moments I am mounting the stone steps by the rock garden and walking along the path toward my front door. Whenever I come back, even after only a few hours' absence, I want to touch each flower and each tree I pass, to tell them something of my joy because I am here with them again. But I think they know it. There is no lamplight to welcome me now, but there is the moon to give a lovelier glow. There are no human voices to call to me, but there is the river's music and the night wind in the trees and all the faint stirrings of woodsy things. Human voices quarrel and say ugly words; human light is not always kind. When I have come back to people, I have expected much and been disapppointed or, not knowing what to expect, I have dreaded the return. But here all is rooted in beauty and in peace and there is surety everywhere. This is home.

5

Commissioner
of trails

What canst thou see elsewhere which thou canst not see here? Behold the heaven and the earth and all the elements; for of these are all things created.

THOMAS a KEMPIS

Watering in July is such a satisfying thing. Each flower and vegetable seems to raise its head in thanks as the cool drops sink into the hot, dry ground. The feathery tops of the carrots are more fairy-like than ever when beaded with moisture and the best leaves glow with a clearer crimson. Watering makes one feel a little like a god.

I do it in the evening when the wind, cool on the warmest day, bends down the bushes and runs along the treetops beside the river. The sun goes down behind the forest, but Cougar and Evergreen mountains are still golden with it. The cabin, with its bark walls looking as though they had grown there, is in shadow. First the sky is cornflower blue, then the paler blue of nemophila, after that the mauve-blue of asperula. At the end it is like only itself and lovelier than any flower. That is when "the star that bids the shepherd fold" comes out and a young moon turns the golden clouds to silver. Later the two tall hemlocks at the Teal edge of my plateau, branching only at their summits, are palm trees on a tropical shore as they stand silhouetted darkly against the argent mountain with the murmuring of water behind them. Light and shadow, shadow and light; from dawn to dawn together they make a glorious world. How strange it must be to see only one and not the other.

July is the prodigal month — of everything except rain — for it is then that black caps, raspberries, blackberries, red elderberries and bitter cherries (tasting of almond) ripen. Bushes and trees bend under the red and dark purple fruit, and mealtime never ends. Rich, tongue-titillating odors stream out of the kitchen where the big preserving pot bubbles and simmers so that the wild berries of the sun may sweeten and warm cold January. Squirrels and chipmunks imitate the "daring young man on the flying trapeze," and Mr. Northwestern Toad of Stump Villa on River Road — "the toad, without which no garden would be complete" — looks phlegmatically at beds blooming with cornflower, viola, snapdragon, hollyhock, carnation, lychnis, godetia, petunia, phlox, viscaria, delphinium, sweet william, agrostemma and half a hundred other blossoms — both wild and tame — of rockery and border. But, best of all to me, there is the prodigality of sun. I can never have enough of it. I stay outside almost every moment of every day, soaking the delicious warmth and light into my body and mind against the coming of those three months of darkness when the sun is only brightness remembered.

It is close and sultry in Home Wood now and the forest has lost the vitality of spring and early summer. The songs of thrush, warbler, sparrow, wren, grosbeak and phoebe have a drowsy quality while the river, shrinking between its banks day by day, is only a sleepy murmuring. The moss is brown on the great boulders beside the Teal, but still green in the deep recesses of the wood where the sun strikes only in narrow shafts between the trunks of the tall evergreens. Bushes meet across the trail at intervals with thimbleberries, black currants and red and blue huckleberries ripening on them while, along the ground, the Oregon grapes are beginning to show their first blue tinge. The sign of bear, deer or sly coyote is on every path and the great horned owl hoots through silver nights that are clear from slim crescent to last quarter.

Bathing in these mountain streams — intentionally, that is — must be restricted to summer, but walking is good at any season. In spring there are trips for exploration of nests and buds, in summer for flowers and berries, in autumn for leaves and wood and in winter for cones and paw prints — and all for beauty.

There is a Ranger for this district, but I have seen him only once, and that was when he came to look over the government land that I subsequently bought. I have, therefore, appointed myself Commissioner of Trails and Wildlife, Secretary of Agriculture, Superintendent of Seasons. One of my duties as Commissioner is to keep the trails open, so I sally out with saw, ax and brush-hook to remove windfalls, bush growth and all impedimenta. November to the end of March is the period of winds. They usually come in the night, and the little cabin creaks and groans and sometimes shakes so violently that I am sure I shall soon find it is no longer attached to earth but sailing over the treetops like the home of Dorothy on the way to Oz. Then I can hear great crashings in the forest — often so close that I am surprised not to see the roof caving in — and know that tomorrow will be a busy day for me on the trails. Occasionally some shakes go flying or pieces of bark are stripped from the outside of the house, but the little place is weathertight — although by no means mouseproof.

All the trees in this district are good Mohammedans — fanatically so, for they not only make the customary obeisance but remain bowing to the east night and day. One of the first things one notices when walking along either of the rivers is how the treetops bend away from the prevailing west wind. When the clouds come riding low and dark along the crest of Fireweed, there is no doubt that a spell of bad weather is on the way. But just at the cabin a frequent little breeze comes from the south — warm in winter, but cool in summer from passing over mountain fields of snow.

I can feel that wind on my right cheek as I wade across Wren River early one July morning,

The day shall not be up so soon as I,
To try the fair adventure of tomorrow.

and climb the bank to Mountain Trail on one of my tours of inspection. Red elderberries flame behind me against a deep blue sky and the scent of flower and ripe fruit is rich on the summer air. A Lewis's woodpecker is swinging it in the groove on a hemlock tree, while far up the Wren I can see Mrs. Barrow's goldeneye whose spouse — together with Messrs. harlequin, merganser et al. — is now enjoying the ocean breezes.

Two members of the calliope family break into commando combat over a patch of purple beard-tongue on the opposite shore, as a violet-green swallow and I depart from that place speedily. We both start along the trail that, at the beginning, parallels the Wren although about a hundred feet above it. It runs along the western flank of Cougar and is very rough and narrow — an icy, treacherous path in winter which needs a clear head and wise feet. There is a cedar plank across a deep gully and, just beyond it, a big fir lying across the path with its head in the river and its roots a hundred feet up the slope. It is something of a landmark and so, as it is possible to get under it, I have never cared to saw a passage through it.

A little farther on, the path turns sharply at right angles and runs east for the rest of the way to Cougar Trail. The junction of the Teal and the Wren is just below me here and Dubh Glas, deep and green, glimmers up at the mountain rising high and dark above me. The trail levels out a little and takes its first steps into the forest, which is still cool and fresh from night. This is an old bed of the Teal and other, older beds can be seen farther up Cougar mountain. In this part of the country during the glacial period many of the valleys were filled with sand, mud and gravel into which streams settled themselves, forming benches and terraces that are now the favorite haunts of prospectors.

Glaciation has made many changes in the topography of this district. Mountaintops have been ground off, underlying rocks polished and less resistant ones furrowed. Glacial grooving — found only in the softer rocks and not at all in the granites — and deposited materials seem to indicate that there was only one period of regional glaciation. But this ice sheet moved large rock fragments considerable distances, as is shown by the occurrence of several tons of Tertiary volcanics not far from my cabin and ten miles from their former resting place on Teal mountain. After the ice cap withdrew, valley and alpine glaciation went on with the work of modification and have continued it until the present. The former remodeled the lowlands, and large glaciers seem to have occupied major valleys for long periods, depositing volumes of eroded materials — of which only a small portion is left now — in the valley bottoms. Meanwhile, the mountain glaciers were changing the form of the higher levels and where they have partially or wholly disappeared, small, clear lakes occupy the depressions that they made. There is one such jewel in the Cocoosh Range, bordered by blue lupine and yellow beard-tongue, which I shall never forget. A few alpine glaciers still remain in this district, but they are not large and should really be called permanent snow fields. The beginning of Mountain Trail lies in the zone of metamorphic and sedimentary rocks: chert, slate and limestone, the oldest of which are products of the Paleozoic age. They are not often found exposed, however, as the terrain is overlaid with gravel.

It is appropriate to think of the Age of Fishes with the river so near. That was also the time of the higher shelled invertebrates, amphibians and primitive flora. Marine life was abundant all through this era, and plant life flourished at the end of it. It is the first great division of time after the appearance of life on this planet. And now we are in the Quatenary era: the Age of Man. When that began there was everything before us. Now we have at least two million years on which to look back and we are still snarling, starving and killing each other for food, territory or whatever represents riches at the time. The tribal battles and the fears of anything strange still go on. We bulk so large in our own eyes that lessons of the past and thoughts of the future are blotted out. I am speaking universally, of course, for we do more than enough trivial worrying about what has been and what will be. Seeing time and the universe whole puts matters in their proper proportion, but that is something which most of us seem unable to do. If we could see even our own world whole and begin to think internationally instead of nationally, then there would be some hope of terminating these famines, pestilences and slaughters that are a disgrace to us as thinking human beings.

Only we so seldom *do* think. It is much easier to be parrots and sheep than men. The individual who actually sits down to work out the truth or falseness of a question is looked upon with a mixture of suspicion and derision. Trying to make us embrace something new — unless, of course, it is some luxury gadget — causes the tasks of Hercules to seem puny by comparison. We draw into our own group, our own country, and everything from outside is looked upon with doubt, if not with enmity. Our advanced men know better, but to the majority a difference in race, color, religion or even politics means a chasm that makes the Grand Canyon seem like a rut in the road. We are so general and so positive in our statements: such and such a man is never to be trusted; these people are all atheists; those are immoral. The reasons for which we condemn our fellow men, without trial or counsel, would horrify us if they were cited in a court of justice. Each person we meet is, as soon as we have had time to ask him a few questions, surrounded by an aura which may have nothing at all in common with his true character. We saddle him with all the judgments that we, in our great wisdom, have made concerning his particular nationality, creed and color. Then we begin to break down those divisions into smaller verdicts: anyone with a high forehead is clever; the person who does not shake hands firmly is deceitful. After that we remember the things our acquaintances have told us about this individual and he is sieved through their prejudiced opinions and ours until there is little left of the original. The reasoning part of our brain is so weak from disuse that we have to depend on all these crutches in order to produce any opinion at all. When we can consider even one soul openly, freely and without bias, there will be some hope for us. When a nation can look upon even one other nation in the same way, there will be some hope for the world.

It is difficult to have small thoughts when walking along a trail that was a river bed thousands of years ago, with the stumps of big trees on either side and other conifers almost as large standing upright and vital. The mountain rises three thousand feet above me. Once it was four thousand feet higher and coated with ice. Perhaps there is still hope for our human sharp corners and glacial intolerance.

I have learned silence from the talkative, toleration from the intolerant, and kindness from the unkind; yet strange, I am ungrateful to those teachers.

The evergreens near the trail are growing so close together that the sun cannot shine through them, but neither can the breeze penetrate to cool the increasing warmth of this July morning. Through hemlock, fir and cedar a wide band of alder, with a few maples and poplars, flares up toward the summit of Cougar. Perhaps the Teal ran here once or perhaps a mountain creek, for moisture still remains and vegetation is plentiful. On a big cedar stump Mrs. Dusky Grouse and one half-grown offspring calmly sit to watch me pass. Bill speaks of two kinds of grouse here: blue and willow. The former are dusky and the latter the ruffed grouse, from my observation. Quail, introduced, are not plentiful in this particular area, but closer to the village all sorts of infants and their mothers can be seen dashing around the underbrush, and autumn brings great whirrings through the trees.

A big Douglas fir beside the path has evidently been a manicuring parlor for cougars; a decaying stump near it is filled with pitch, and I break it apart to fill two burlap bags with material for quick, hot fires. Here is an old shaft, driven by prospectors, and the ladder that belonged to it. Everywhere in these parts are the traces of men who dug and panned for gold in the old days, but few signs of their descendants, who now search for the precious minerals of strategy, although several of the latter — platinum, lead, zinc, aluminum, chromium, tungsten and manganese — have been found in this locality.

The path begins to climb and, very gradually, to drift inland. The river is just a whispering far below. Miner's lettuce, bedstraw and twinflower riot over the ground, and sword fern clumps are scattered here and there. Small evergreens — among them Douglas fir, western hemlock, yew, grand fir, giant cedar, Sitka spruce and one or two yellow cypress (although there are no real stands of the last-named at this altitude of around two thousand feet) — have sprung up in legions, and between them the prickly devil's club thrusts its scarlet head. Looking at it, I can understand how the Indians came to use it so often in their ceremonial medicine. It is surely the strange, grotesque medicine man of these tribes of forest flowers.

The trail is smooth and hard — for the smaller streams that

trickle down the mountain during other seasons are dry now —
and so I have, as yet, found little use for my woodcutting imple-
ments. Dogbane, which gave the Indians fibers for fishnets and
from whose milky juice india rubber can be made, and the waxy
pink blossoms of pear-leaved wintergreen appear beside The
Canoe — a large-girthed cedar, hollowed out by fire, which lies
across the path.

Going or coming, I can never resist lying down in it, with my
head in a slight depression, and looking up at the green, waving
branches overhead. Like Montaigne, "I have ever loved to repose myself, whether sitting or lying, with my heels as high as
or higher than my head." It is more open here and a cool breeze
drifts up from the river. The lovely notes of the varied thrush
come drifting on the air — "there is a good deal of fragmentary
conversation going on among the birds, even on the warmest
days" — and a little later I am startled to hear the characteristic
melody of Townsend's solitaire. This elusive singer of the mountains usually frequents higher places and I was not even aware
that he was an inhabitant of these particular hills. I would like to
meet him. He and I should have much in common, for we both
prefer the solitary life and find great happiness in it.

Not that I am allergic to people. I cannot think of one person
whom I actually dislike and for humanity in general I care, I
believe, a great deal more than those who hold that many acquaintances indicate great love of one's fellow man and who are
never contented away from the crowd. Yet these same compla-
cent ones will betray friendship and stab their acquaintances
with malicious gossip and when it comes to the test, the truth
finally appears that they love no one but themselves. This may
seem like a very jaundiced observation from one as particularly
blessed with friends as I, for I can name seven on whom I can
call at any time and they will do for me whatever is humanly
possible. They and I can communicate without words and when
we are together, walls and cities fall away, and it might be that
great first morning of the world. I feel very humble when I think
of it.

I am sure, however, that I would not care as much for that

first universal morning as I do for the dawns that tap at my window now when

> *Night's candles are burnt out, and jocund day*
> *Stands tiptoe on the misty mountain-tops.*

There would have been no thrush in it, no pale pink twinflower, no tall evergreen for shade and delight, but only hot winds and titanic downpours of rain, with lava underfoot and a great sun and moon moving across a storm-wracked sky with earthquakes behind them. The severest climate of this present world would be mild and beneficent in comparison, but now there are the earthquakes of war, the storms of pestilence, the killing winds of famine that go on not only undiminished but increased by some of the great "benefits" of civilization. We save with one hand and destroy with the other. We seem able to change everything but ourselves. But that we *can* change, I know. When I consider the person I was when I first came to these mountains, I know that something like a miracle has taken place. Now I am, although far from what I hope to be, capable of living with nature unashamed. I can go with a clear heart along this trail, feeling kinship with everything that surrounds me — as I do with everything living, human or otherwise, that is trying to reach up to those stars, "unutterably bright," which shine for all of us. How we do it does not matter, but that we *do* it is of the utmost importance.

I remember when I first came here. The mountains made me feel so small and when the night fell, the forests seemed to threaten me with their greater darkness. I knew with Victor Hugo that "there is a sacred horror about everything grand. It is easy to admire mediocrity and hills; but whatever is too lofty, a genius as well as a mountain, an assembly as well as a masterpiece, seen too near, is appalling." Here was I, one little human being in all this immensity of hilled and timbered space; no neighbor for over four miles, no village for twenty, no large town for more than a hundred. Mountains, rivers and forests were not strangers to me, for I had seen them in almost every state and province of North America, in Hawaii, Europe and faraway places, but always surrounded by people and with cities everywhere. So now all this, to live in for my lifetime if all went well, seemed more than I could bear. I did not realize that I was like a starving man who has suddenly been given more food than his stomach can tolerate; like someone whose body has become so inured to poison that purity revolts it. First I must cleanse myself, then I must renew. Then, and not until then, could I look my mountains calmly in the face and know that the kingdom of heaven was indeed within me — if I would only let it be.

How could it be otherwise when there is so much beauty everywhere: in the small blue flowers of peavine and the green-white blossoms of the round-leaved orchis; in the lilting cadences of the hidden warbling vireo and the olive-white flash of a Traill's flycatcher. Certainly the Park, on Mountain Trail, is one of the lovely places of the world. It is a broad area of cedar trees and stumps, ground vines and emerald moss, with practically no underbrush in any part of it. There may have been a lake here in old days, or perhaps it was simply a widening of the Teal. However it was then, it is beautiful now, with sunlight filtering through the cedar branches and patterning moss and flower into a carpet more exquisite than any out of Persia. False azalea with its honeysuckle-scented leaves is there, with yellow monkey-flower and moonwort in rare, small clumps.

There is no sound but the faint sibilance of the river, the clear note of the black-throated gray warbler and the winged whisper of a calliope hummingbird above late blooming columbine. My heart is not large enough to hold all this beauty and eternity would be far too short a time to fill my eyes with it! It is like the strange fairy palaces I used to imagine as a child — always green or sparkling white — and the unspoken dreams of adolescence, like that shining glimpse of the Holy Grail that sometimes comes in later years. They are all here, somewhere — in this cool and odorous place perfumed by flower, wood, bracken and moist earth. I walk through it slowly, reluctant to leave and making many little side trips of exploration.

Just as I step out of the Park and start down a short hill to the salmonberry flats beyond, I realize that something or someone is just ahead of me. I catch the flicker of a branch coming upward after weight, the quiver of a leaf where there is no wind and see that some salmonberries — which are at their ripest now on this northern slope — have been freshly picked. Then a grunt, an acrid smell, the sound of rolling stones, and a black bear and I are looking at each other. The tableau holds for perhaps a minute and then with a sniff, a whoof and much crashing through the underbrush the breakfaster ambles up the mountain. About fifty feet away he stops to peer at me and I see a comical sight: a black bear balanced on a log with all four feet bunched together, looking like a cross between a near-sighted old gentleman and a trained seal on a ball! It is all I can do not to laugh, but I would not hurt his dignity for anything — especially as I have so rudely interrupted the fruit course of his morning meal.

Down in the salmonberry flat I realize that it is a hot day. The bushes have spread tremendously since I was here in April and now arch over my head as I cut my way through them. This is no place for anyone with a leaning toward claustrophobia, for the air is heavy and humid and the swampy trail is hard to find. There are huge cedar stumps here also, but hardly any living evergreens. Black cottonwoods, aspens, red alders, Hooker willows, vine and broadleaf maples are plentiful and there is even one western birch, the only living one that I have found near this trail. The stinging nettles (pity the poor princess!) are bad and the deer flies are worse, but it is impossible to hurry. I remember an acquaintance who said that living in a valley — in his case the valley of the Bow River in Canada — had given him acute claustrophobia and I wonder how he would have liked this. It is difficult for me to understand how such a wide valley as the one he knew could have that effect, yet he declared that the mountains seemed to press in on him and that when he looked straight ahead he could never see the sky. But surely it is good to have to look up.

On this trail both climate and terrain change very quickly. The swamp turns into a hill and the hill into a wide, dry flat with flowers — violet fleabane, yellow stonecrop and purple sanicle — which I had previously found only in quite arid places. I see where the engraver beetle — called "Chinese bug" locally — has been at his destructive work, and in the crevices of another tree trunk I find the bark beetle doing his helpful best to clear away fungus. I wonder if the latter knows how much he resembles a

bedbug and how many deaths in his large family must have resulted from that fact. A large snail is lying in the path and I catch a swift, red-striped glimpse of a Puget Sound garter snake whisking along the ground.

Several trees have fallen across the trail here, so it is nearly noon when I go on again — this time following along a creek bed which has water still lying in it. Salmonberries are plentiful, and I eat my first luncheon course when I have finished cutting their parent bushes back from the path. A dozen of these berries swallowed together are as satisfying as a draught of cold water and that fact does much to make up for their lack of flavor. My way runs almost at river level here, and the Teal — although it is impossible to see it — makes a big outward curve at this point. A belt of greenstone — chiefly augite andesites, but including slates and sediments — begins now and extends for about a mile beyond the point where Mountain and Cougar trails meet.

There is then an abrupt transition from greenstone, in which very little serpentinization has appeared, into pure serpentine. Quite a number of these swift changes take place in this district, the serpentine areas usually being very irregular in outline and generally occurring near fracture zones. In the area surrounding Bill's property there are numerous quartz veins in the cherty rocks, while both chert and slate are intersected on occasion by rhyolite or diorite porphyry dikes. Massive greenstone is here also and in its neighborhood many small tourmaline crystals have been found. The large pink crystals of exinite have also been discovered and the dark-blue and light pebbles of chert conglomerate.

I have come across many pieces of serpentine and the appearance of that green-gray rock is then quite different from that of the highly polished stones used for ornament. I have found it most frequently in shades of green, but it can also be brown-yellow, brown-red and sometimes almost white. It is a metamorphic magnesian rock, soft enough to cut with a knife and of a pearly luster. The small stones that have been smoothed by river action are quite lovely.

Now the trail, with the ghost-white stems of Indian pipe beside it, climbs steeply into the evergreen forest again. Placer Pike ends — or begins, if you like — here, angling sharply up Cougar mountain past a cabin and camp of Bill's, through miles of blackened stumps along the ridge, passing the road to Chert Lake and finally meeting Gold Road far up beyond the Cocoosh Range. A branch of Placer Pike strikes down from the top of Cougar to the Wren, almost opposite my cabin. It is a very steep path that, when slippery, tends toward a great deal of backsliding.

The scourge of fire lashes this country each summer, with September usually being the peak month. It has not come very near my property for a long time, but each year the air is bitter and blue with smoke, and gray-white puffs of it show up over Fireweed and Evergreen. I watch them anxiously until the rains begin.

So many of these conflagrations are started by sheer carelessness, although it is necessary here to have a fire permit from May until October. But even prospectors, versed as they are in the ways of the woods, have their thoughtless moments, and the less principled among them have been known to set fire to the bush deliberately in order to expose the rocks and so make the location of minerals easier. Property and even life — unless belonging to themselves — mean nothing to such men. We find them everywhere — disregarding the rights of others, slandering them, running the black markets, selling worthless stock. They are among the governing and the governed, and a bit of them seems to exist in all of us. When we borrow something and misuse it; when we try to profit from a national emergency; when we carry tales and institute malicious gossip. Women are supposed to be greater gossips than men, but when men are together they yield the palm to no one. Gossip has two intertwined roots: envy and a feeling of inferiority. Women have always been made to feel inferior, and that may be why they delight in the tales which give them a sense of superiority, both over their unfortunate victim and over their uninformed listeners. Men often feel inferior to other men and so compete to hold the floor, if only for a short interval, with a spicy yarn concerning common acquaintances. Or perhaps everyone else is doing it and they *must* be a "good fellow." If they did not feel inferior, there would be no reason for them to be anything but themselves.

If I should ever erect a "No Trespass" sign on my property, it would read: "Not welcome here: those who are not kind." It is so simple to be kind, although it may be difficult to know the kindest thing to do in a given situation. Yet two precepts show us the way: "Know thyself" and "This above all to thine own self be true." But first we must find out who we really are. The tendency these days — raised to the nth degree in dictators — is to develop as hard a skin as possible and then ride roughshod over others. We scorn those who are sensitive — not "touchy"! — and retiring; we delight in hurting them if we think they cannot strike back. Dreamers and idealists are considered to be so much rubbish to be scrapped as soon as possible. Yet every good thing we have had to be dreamed first. If there had been all doers and no thinkers in this world, we would probably still be eating raw meat and dressing in skins. With all thinkers and no doers we would have died out long ago.

But that better world of the dreamers must have a different pattern of life from that of past years. There must be no children starving while crops are plowed under; no adults committing suicide from preventable despair; no poverty-stricken old age after a life of work; no sickness neglected because of poverty; no persecutions because of race, creed or color. We must clean our house and clean it thoroughly.

Some of this may come about through laws proposed by a few intelligent individuals, but the main body of it must come through the minds of the people. That means that we must change our ways of thinking about many things. Thought is actually the strongest power in the world, but so few of us realize it. So many times and in so many countries we have seen the power of mass thought when directed toward evil ends; is it logical to think that it would be any less strong if turned into channels for good? Yet when I mention these things to acquaintances, I am laughed at and told that I am a visionary. They say that what I suggest cannot even be done — but never having tried it, how can they know? Nations are nothing more than collections of individuals. If we, one by one, begin to change our thinking, then the day will inevitably come when the nation will go the good way we wish it to go and no other. Whenever those popular words of Carl Schurz are quoted: "Our country, right or wrong," the phrases immediately following are apparently forgotten: "When right, to be kept right; when wrong, to be put right." As the people will, the nation will go; as the nations will, the world will go.

It is no little thing to change even one bad habit in ourselves for we can never know how far our influence may travel. "A word fitly spoken is like apples of gold in pictures of silver." Even in this so-called wilderness I am not alone. My writing goes out into the world and speaks for me. I must be careful of what it says, careful not to make things appear other than they are, but to see that they are good in the first instance. If my inner living is wrong, then word piled upon word will not conceal it. If my inner living is right, then even if I have broken a convention or a bad law it will not matter. Conventions change, and those that are right for some may not be right for all. As for bad laws, I think that they should be broken again and again until they have been forced from the statute books. They strike at the very foundations of democracy: that each may live according to his own ideas as long as he does not intefere with the rights of others. They breed disrespect for all law.

The brown creeper on a hemlock beside me is evidently not a democratic citizen for he is undoubtedly interfering with the rights of several insects. He flies down a trail leading to some old logging cabins by the river and I follow him. This by-path is a lovely little one with buttercups, bluebells, oyster plant, yellow wood sorrel and butterfly leaf growing beside it and vine maples bending over it. In the clearing surrounding the cabins the creamy birch-leaved spirea borders a glorious clump of the tall mauve foxglove, and the whole appears almost like a conventional garden. But on a small bank, just where the bush begins again, is the loveliest sight of all: masses of one-flowered wintergreen with its pink-hooded blossoms and white-veined leaves. This is the only place on these trails where I have found this charming little flower and the sight is one I shall never forget.

Milfoil, or yarrow, with its fern-like leaves is here also. Achilles used it to heal the wounds of his warriors at the siege of Troy, and all through the ages it has figured in the folklore of the countryside as a cure for everything from lovesickness to toothache. When I discovered that it is used in Sweden as a substitute for hops, I mourned for its classic past of love philter and restoring unguent! Another Grecian namesake grows beside the milfoil: wild mint, called after the Greek nymph who was fabled to have been changed into that plant. Our grandparents made peppermint tea from its leaves — the oil from this plant is also used commercially — and so, when the dark winter days arrive, do I. The delicate green liquid in a pale yellow cup never fails to bring spring to my dining-table. The flavor resembles the blossom tea of China and is, in my opinion, infinitely preferable to that of our black variety.

In the clearing surrounding some deserted cabins and at the border of the river are the slender-stemmed water leaf and the pink monkey-flower. The leaves of clustered dock appear gigantic beside the tiny heart-shaped ones of shepherd's-purse, which are such lovely duplicates in shape of the wallets oldtime shepherds used to carry.

Fortunately for all gardeners, horsetail and ragwort are rare — although they both appear near these cabins and mine — for they spread with the speed of light and fight root and stock against removal. The former, which is a cryptogam and propagates through spores and not by seed, has been successfully used for experiments in the location of gold deposits. It is systematically collected over large areas and spectroscopically examined, so that very minute quantities of the element can be easily detected. This method is used for finding both base and precious metals, as concentrations of the element in plants — horsetail has a particular affinity for gold — are indicative of the proximity of the element in the ground. The only competitor of ragwort and horsetail in the matter of tenacity and growth is the crabgrass, or fingergrass, which crops up cheerfully in any garden. It was naturalized from Europe and the great regret of anyone who has made its acquaintance is that it ever left that continent. It is one alien we could do without.

Purple copper and reaper dart butterflies color the clear, warm air as I eat my lunch on a cabin doorstep, and a hover fly hesitates above the many flowers. A "ladybird" alights on my hand and I sing to it the old children's rhyme: "Ladybug, Ladybug, fly away home!" which originated in the burning of the hop vines and cranberry plants in fall when eggs, larvae and young beetles died in the flames while their parents flew away from the holocaust. Bees bumble comfortably through the clearing, and a swarm of crane flies suddenly appears from nowhere and as suddenly goes again. Red ants are swarming near a rotten stump, but I never take much pleasure in watching them. Their ruler-soldier-slave system is too much like that of dictators, who employ the same method in building up their state. Their tactics in obtaining slave workers, i.e., raiding other countries (nests) and forcibly carrying off the inhabitants, resemble those of the warrior-ants who carry off unhatched cocoons so that the inmates may be used as slaves when they emerge. All the great activity of the ant, so lauded in books, seems to me nothing more than the busyness of rulers and soldiers enforcing the busyness of workers, foragers and slaves.

I find the higher coolness of Mountain Trail very pleasant when I climb back to it again. From here to Cougar Trail I shall probably have no use for ax or brush-hook as Bill keeps the way cleared to Placer Pike, which I have just passed. Soon the path dips sharply down and I find myself scrambling over creeks and morasses, jumping from log to log and finally going in over my boot-tops. Because of the late spring and hard winter, the larger brooks are still running and they talk to each other as they gleam past mossy boulder and through masses of the lovely silver-backed fern starred with miterwort and twinflower. Coolness blows up from the waters of Cougar Creek, which runs all the year every year, and I lean on the tiny log bridge to watch the sparkling of baby waterfalls and the clear, dark flowing of deeper places. This stream has come a long way from the summit of Cougar, but it is as alive and joyous as ever as it laughs up at the dark evergreens and then leaps away through the underbrush to its meeting with the Teal.

Just before the junction with Cougar Trail there is a wide, dry flat with a cabin on it where other neighbors lived in other years. Bill and I have fallen heir to the fruit of their bushes, and sometimes I carry away wild catnip leaves to use in place of sage.

Ocean spray and the lovely rose-red flowers of hardhack — whose other name of steeplebush I much prefer — border this clearing, with nipplewort and St.-John's-wort adding to its sunshine. Cougar Trail itself is like a garden with buttercup, blue beard-tongue, purple hedge nettle, yellow compass plant, honeysuckle, spiraea, another species of miner's lettuce and — surprise! surprise! — some blue calico flowers in pink calico dresses, looking like strawberry sundaes with a touch of chocolate sauce.

The way is cleared, the sun is hot so I, Commissioner of Trails and Wildlife, after an interesting conversation with a MacGillivray warbler, amble across the long Teal bridge (which seems to have every intention of going down to the Mallard on the next flood) and up the farther slope to have a cup of Labrador tea with Bill.

Small cheer and great welcome makes a merry feast.

6

High mountains
are
a feeling

And the wooded sides of the mountain appear; and from the
  heavens an infinite ether is diffused
And all the stars are seen.

HOMER

Sleeping out underneath the summer stars is an experience not quite like any other. There is at the same moment a feeling of constant movement and of utter stillness, of the warmth of beauty and the chill of infinite space. I am conscious as never before of the greatness of humanity, and yet I realize how small a seed it is dropped down on this tiny plot of the immeasurable gardens of the universe.

I spend nearly all the summer nights outdoors, with my sleeping bag unrolled on the lawn, on the borders of Home Wood or down on the flat beside the Teal. I watch the baleful red eye of Mars and the cold green glance of Vega move across the darkened sky and I see the Great Bear swing lower and lower over Fireweed. But one August night I am not satisfied with this, for Ursa Minor has reminded me of the little black bears who haunt the shores of Wren River at berry time and I feel in my bones that the wild black currants are ripe.

So the next morning, just as the sun is climbing over Cougar, I tie sleeping bag, cooking utensils, ax, brush-hook, fly rod, berry pails and food — very little of the last named for I shall find fish and fruit wherever I go on this journey — on my packboard and go down the path to the Wren between the guardian bushes of pink and white heather. African daisies, nasturtiums and asperula overflow the two stumps which stand just at the top of the bank with the stillness of early morning on them. A red admiral butterfly flits over the flowers and a tiger swallowtail passes me like flickering sunlight. I glimpse a red crest and know that the dramatic pileolated woodpecker is coming to the hemlock on the knoll for breakfast. A Wright's flycatcher skims across the soft red fruit of the thimbleberry bushes and all my other feathered neighbors sing matins in their own charming way.

The river talks to itself, softly at first and then louder and louder as I navigate the short, steep bank and stand at water level. My scrambling has disturbed a pygmy owl who, with one amazed look in my direction, flaps peevishly up the river. The silence of his going makes me wish that man might have soft, airtight wings also — especially in moments of anger. A Richardson's pewee flits up from a branch above my rinsing pool — rinsing being a simple matter of holding the clothes in the swift current of the river until the soap has disappeared — and a belted kingfisher screams angrily as I mount the Wren River cage from its platform of a single log and shake the steel cable on which he has been posing so magnificently.

There is a feeling of adventure in swinging out over the swift water like this with only two narrow boards — for this cage is smaller than the one for Teal River — between me and the stream racing by below. The sun glints from the rocks and strikes sparks from the ripples, while a tepid breeze comes down from the uplands, which have lain in warmth since dawn. Everything looks so fresh and clear after the cleansing dews of night, and the air has a gloss to it. Any journey is exciting and this one, although I have taken it many times, never loses its zest for me. Why should it? Each time I find something new: a bird, a flower or a strange stone upon the shore. There is the trip upstream by the river, the night beside it and the journey over Ipo and Rue mountains with a night by some small clear lake of a high alpine meadow or perhaps near a waterfall of the high forests. Then there is the final stretch, across and down Cougar, with fish on a string and pounds of pungent currants. Perhaps a black bear and I will find ourselves picking from the same bush or, lying awake in the night, I shall hear the coyotes howling in the dry uplands, or none of these happenings at all — but others as rich and rare.

The other side of the river is in shadow, and I can feel coolness rising up from the moist earth. The way along the shore is of sand and gravel, with rock-jumping a great feature of it. My boots are slung around my neck and my costume consists of shirt and shorts — with the shirt soon to be discarded. It will be almost a miracle if I meet anyone, for those few who fish the lower Wren — and I shall not go as far as the upper reachers — must pass my cabin, and no one has done so within the last few days. Fishermen from outside are now few and far between, although they used to be fairly plentiful. I am not so sorry as I might be about this dearth, for I shall not easily forget the "sportsmen" who dynamited the pool, Dubh Glas, one day when I was absent and left the shores littered with dead trout that they could not carry away with them. Or the ones who swaggered down the Wren with three times the legal catch and boasted that next summer they would come back with "sticks" for Chert Lake.

The rock formations along the Wren are principally chert, slate and limestone, but, as elsewhere in this district, so overlaid with gravel that little of the original shows through. Farther along, the river runs through a serpentine belt and then through one that is chiefly slate. It branches there toward the two mountain springs that are its sources, twenty miles above the juncture with the Teal. There is no human habitation in all that way and when I travel it, I feel like an explorer first setting foot in some strange Erewhon. But, of course, it is not unknown, for evidences of past placer operations show at intervals and, near the course, Gold Road crosses it running east and west through the Cocoosh and Endahwin country. It is in these two mountain groups that the branches of the river originate. The Cocoosh branch runs, at this beginning, through a region which is rolling and open, but the Endahwin fork tears down between steep canyon walls to the lower lands beyond.

There is also a canyon near the outlet of the Wren. I can see the entrance to it now as I boulder-jump along the margin of the sunlit stream with willow, aspen, cottonwood, alder and maple touching me gently as I go by. Just across from me the sluice boxes begin, which carry water into my dam to be pumped up to the tank by ram. Purple fleabane, foamflower, miner's lettuce and yellow avens give the whole a tropical, exotic appearance.

The dark, mysterious berries of black nightshade are almost ripe and I register that fact with nightshade pies in mind. Many people confuse this plant with that of the deadly nightshade from which atropine is made and so refuse to eat the really delicious fruit. The Indians once considered the red huckleberry to be poisonous and would not eat it even when they were starving, while I have had people — and books — tell me that the red elderberry could not be eaten without danger.

Thinking of the many jars of red elderberry jelly — made with orange, lemon or rose hip juice to add pectin and flavor — I have consumed since coming here, I find these tales very amusing. The red berries of devil's club and baneberry are, I believe, the only fruit I have not sampled. The blue berries of salal and alpine beauty, the red fruit of false solomon's seal, twisted-stalk and starflower, the golden fruit of fairy bells — all these go into my preserving pot, together with more conventional products. I believe that I am still alive, although some of my acquaintances seem to doubt it.

Just beyond a smaller dam — which marks the entrance to my irrigation system — is one of my favorite bathtubs. Shallow, warm and surrounded by large rocks through which a current of fresh water flows continuously, it is irresistible. Afterward I let the sun dry me as I sit, steeped in animal content, on a boulder of velvet moss. Time and space swing free for a moment. There is no beginning and no end, but only this *being* of warmth and peace and the mesmerism of water. For these few moments I can grasp the ultimate essentials of life. Here I am, one human soul, with my bed, my food, my small ax and matches for fire and my rod to add to sustenance. What more could I possibly want — and even a rod is not necessary as a branch would do as well. A book? Marcus Aurelius is in the pocket of the jacket I have brought for evening warmth and I could read him for months on end without exhausting his wisdom or being myself exhausted. He is mentor and unswerving friend and can give me in one paragraph more than many of the souls "outside" can give me in a lifetime.

Each time I go "outside," it is as though I stepped from a land of freedom into a country of captivity. Everyone there seems to be a slave: to possessions, ambition, fear, envy or the trivial minutiae of wasted hours. They feel that they cannot do this or that because of their job, their money or their reputation. They are bound by the chains of opinion and material ownership, and their conversation is a series of complaints against their employers or employees, their neighbors, the government and any other person or thing that they can find to blame for their discontent. Like Gratiano, their reasons are "as two grains of wheat hid in two bushels of chaff; you shall seek all day ere you find them, and when you have them, they are not worth the search." They have never bothered to sit down and try to analyze their unhappiness — even if they were capable of doing so, which is doubtful — and they have certainly never heard the saying: "A man may fall many times, but he is only a failure when he begins to blame others."

They believe that if only they have more money, a larger house or a different wife or husband, then the zenith of joy will be reached and they will never be unhappy again. Of course it is not true and sometimes, perhaps in that lost hour before the dawn, there may be a whisper in their hearts that tells them so. But with daylight it is gone and once more they are reaching out with hooked, insistent fingers toward the material treasures of their little, little world. But where is their world in time? They have no sense of the future beyond material safeguards for themselves and their children, while the "treasures in heaven" would be rated on a par with shares in a wildcat mine. Yet neither do they live in the present, for today is only a steppingstone to the greater possessions of tomorrow and so to be passed over as swiftly as possible.

These people really live in a nonexistent world of their own which can be blown away at any moment — and is being blown away at this moment — in which there is nothing solid, nothing enduring, nothing successful in the true meaning of those words. Think back over those who were called failures by former generations — the struggling and scorned poets, musicians, artists, scholars, philosophers, scientists — and think how many of them now receive our adulation.

Seven cities warred for Homer being dead,
Who living had no roof to shroud his head.

But where are the great moguls of business and politics who were feted and adored by their contemporaries? Lethe has covered them; only those show above the flood who had something beyond that which their fellow citizens called success. For if one thing is truer than any other, it is that the unmaterial things of life are the only solid and enduring ones.

If ever a generation should know that truth, it is this generation. Half the people of the world have lost some or all of those possessions without which they felt they could not live, and the other half will be stripped down to bare essentials before many years have passed. Only character can come out of this holocaust enriched and strengthened; can go on with faith and courage to build better than before. If these years of ice and flame can teach the many what the few know now and what Christ knew nearly two thousand years ago: "What is a man profited if he shall gain the whole world, and lose his own soul?", then they will not have been in vain.

We may have to face tomorrow with only those possessions that we can carry on our backs — and if those are all we have we shall perish. But if we can lose even those few things and still step forward undismayed, then we are greater than Alexander, and Midas is a beggar beside us. Comfort? What is comfort to us if we are already spiritually dead when we attain it? Who told us that comfort was the meaning of existence or that it could ever bring us happiness? To it we have made sacrifices which stink to heaven: integrity, honor, happiness, peace, freedom. It has chained our hearts and imprisoned our minds so that in time we become too weak and too blinded to walk upright in the light of day.

Verily the lust for comfort murders the passion of the soul and then walks grinning in the funeral.

My enemies call me a failure and my acquaintances shake their heads scornfully over my lack of "success." Only my friends realize that the times I have failed most bitterly were those in which I tried to "do right" in the eyes of the world. Now I have a few books, fewer clothes, food that I grow myself and fuel that I cut with my own hands; there is a roof over my head that I helped to build and earth under my feet that I have cultivated. Every material thing has been swept away or reduced to its simplest elements in order to clear the path for "plain living and high thinking." In coming close to earth I have come close to heaven.

Whatever life may be to others, this is life to me. Even if I should lose my cabin and the ground which I have built up so carefully; even if I were forced to go on with only the few things I have with me here by this rock on the Wren, yet I would go on courageously and hopefully, in full belief that my richest treasures were still in my possession. Any day you or I or all of us may be left with empty hands; let us be sure that such a day will find us with full minds and hearts.

But what of too many others — what will they do then? Some will be completely demoralized and go, whining still, to their graves and to their lost hope of heaven. Some will feverishly clutch what remains to them materially and watch slyly for a chance to rob others. Some may revolt to regain what they have lost or to obtain what they never had. A few, stripped of the worthless coverings that hid them from themselves, may ponder the truth of that saying of Robert Jones Burdette's: "What you wish you were, that is your ideal. What people say you are, that is your reputation. What you know you are, that is your character." They may realize at last that what the world acclaims as right and honorable may be a great wall dividing man from God.

It all seems very simple, here on this rock beside the Wren, and I feel that I could not be doing a better thing than turning such thoughts over in my mind and writing them down so that what worth there is in them may be shared with you. For you are here with me, you who read these lines! The sun is in your face and the breeze from the uplands is wandering through your hair. There is a day before us and a night to come when we shall live intimately with soil and sky and know the interweaving of earth and heaven. We are alive — we are living at last!

Just beyond the bathing pool a tiny falls chatters away invitingly, with blue-eyed Mary and rough bedstraw stirring above me on the bank. A red-tailed hawk idles overhead and a black-winged grasshopper leaps along the sandy shore. I am at the beginning of the first small canyon whose west wall is the side of Evergreen mountain and whose east is the flank of Cougar mountain. The stones here are great boulders, for this part seems to have been one of the playing fields of the Titans. Their huge balls are strewn everywhere and in the defrosting days of spring I can hear, from my cabin, rollings and crashings of sound as more and more of them hurtle down mountain walls to the stream bed below.

The whole four miles of this canyon are studded with waterfalls and creeks which plunge almost perpendicularly down from the heights above. Many of the smaller streams are dry in summer, but in August there are still enough left to moisten the soil on both sides of the river and encourage the delicate fairy bells (now bright with the salmon-colored berries that have given the plant its other name of "gold drops"), blue beard-tongue, yellow monkey-flower and the late wild rose to grow in delicate loveliness. Jerusalem oak is here with false dandelion and waterleaf. The spicy scent of wild black currants pricks the air, and prickly blackberry vines lay snares for the unwary foot. But I shall not fill my pails until the day after tomorrow.

A hurly-burly little five-foot falls gives luncheon music where a black cap bush loaded with berries — but soon unloaded — overhangs the rock which is my table. Deer flies and sand flies overhang it also and when I get up to go on I, like peace, have slain my "ten thousands." A dipper accompanies me out of the canyon and a song sparrow waves its tail in greeting. I pass crystal pools where I can see the fish distinctly, and it is almost more than I can do to go by. But there will be other pools, and three or four brook trout are more than enough for supper and breakfast — even though I know "angling to be like the spirit of humility, which has a calmness of spirit and a world of other blessings attending on it."

Cedars, firs, hemlocks and many deciduous trees have greened the sides of the canyon, but now on the east bank burned stumps and blackened shells begin to appear, coming in some places right down to the water's edge. Soon both sides show these ruins, the mountains begin to recede and the river forgets its haste to meander slowly through meadowlands where only cindered trunks mark the graves of forest giants. It must have been very beautiful here before this fire of fourteen years ago, and even now the rib grass, common plantain and two species of willow herb are doing their best to cover unsightly scars. These willow herbs and especially the giant fireweed, are citizens of the world and have been celebrated through generations. The Indians have many stories concerning the fireweed, which they would tell as they scraped out the contents of the stalks and ate them or relished the tender young shoots and leaves that were such a welcome change from winter fare. It makes all places beautiful with its tall spike of rose-purple flowers; even the bombed and devastated areas of old London were transmuted into loveliness by the "willowweed."

Where there is any moisture in this burned section by the Wren, growth is luxuriant, but in many places the topsoil has been damaged so badly that nothing has flowered there since. Gaunt rocks protrude at intervals while high and higher gravel benches — in which heavy rains and spring thaws have gouged great holes — can be seen rising into the distance. The river winds in soft curves and in the background the mountains, denuded also of great timber, rise toward the sun with the Peak of God's Fools to the south, higher than all the others.

The height of this flat is twelve feet above the river and with a slight slope toward it. There is a burned cabin on the west bank with fire-blackened heads of crowbars, spades, picks and other tools projecting from the soil around it. Half a mile farther on are the ruins of another cabin, this time on the east bank, with a faint trail passing it and small black cap bushes springing up around what was once the doorway. A deer trail comes down to the water, and just beyond is a trapper's lean-to with boards where marten traps stood. The river begins to narrow again and then enters another canyon, but one in which the walls are only about a hundred feet high. These walls come closer and closer until finally all the August water of the Wren is pouring between them in three feet of space.

Green timber begins again at the other side and, the sun westering, I begin to look for a camping site. An open place on the east bank catches my eye for there is a large flat rock in front of it where I can build my permitted fire and from which I can fish in the clear, deep pool below. Soon I am practicing the "calm, quiet, innocent recreation of angling" and not long afterward two Dolly Vardens are lying, filleted, in my frying pan. Two more are refrigerated for breakfast, and a sluice box screen which I picked up at one of the burned cabins (everyone in this country becomes a pack rat of discarded property) is supported on stones and suspended over the flames. It is large enough to hold my frying pan, a tin plate on which cornmeal cakes are rising and a berry pail in which I first boil garden-fresh peas and then water for coffee. Two large ears of corn, still wrapped in their husks, are roasting in the ashes, and black caps are heaped on broadleaf maple leaves.

While supper is cooking, I cut cedar boughs to place under my sleeping bag and make things shipshape for the night. Because of the more open country, the sun stays longer here than it does back at the cabin, but it will soon be down behind the western mountains and then the chill of forest and river will come creeping up to make me put on more clothing and sit closer to my fire. It is very warm there, for after starting with birch and cedar I have piled on maple and alder for a hot enduring flame. There was, of course, no necessity to use green wood, for windfalls are everywhere, while I could have begun my fire just as readily with twigs and carried it on with hemlock — if not too wet — and fir. Cottonwood has both heat and staying power, but its windfalls are usually so water-soaked that much time and a big blaze is needed to dry them.

As I sit drinking fragrant coffee, night moves slowly but inexorably down the mountains and along the river. The first star appears and a small, cool evening wind stirs gently. The sky darkens and more stars come out, but there will be no moon until early morning. A spider has been spinning his silver threads above my sleeping bag, not far from a silver-gray cocoon of the whirligig bug. A swarm of crane flies has watched the sunset with me and a dagger moth flutters near the blaze. By the time I have washed the dishes and myself, stars and fire are the only lights in the darkness around me. I crawl into my sleeping bag and lie there looking up at the gem-encrusted heavens.

It is not "the stars inviting to slumber" but, with Virgil again

As when the mind of man who has come over much earth,
Sallies forth, and he reflects with rapid thoughts,
There was I, and there, and remembers many things. . . .

For my mind is filled with images of other nights: beside another fire in the Bitterroot Range with staked-out pack horses snuffling softly in the darkness beyond; riding down from Yellowstone Park toward the lights of Cody on a half-bronco with suicidal tendencies and the hardest mouth I have ever encountered; beside a swift river of the Siskiyous and a lazy bayou of Louisiana; in a tent on a Pennsylvania farm and in a cabin high up in the Santa Clara Mountains of California; lying on a warm beach of the Pacific; and feeling Atlantic sand grow cold beneath me as I watched the waves fringe the dark ocean with lustered white. Nights spent in every state of the United ones: eastern nights with the full grass flavor of summer in them; hot, dry nights of the Middle West with "nothing that rises marring the level miles, but all for the seeing seen"; nights in the Nebraska hills; beside Echo Lake in the high mountains of Colorado; in a car caught fast in Missouri mud or the red clay of Georgia; near a zinc mine of Oklahoma, a turquoise mine of New Mexico, a silver mine of Nevada, or a gold "mine" of Alaska; driving through the bleakness of the Dakota badlands, the piney woods of Mississippi, the vast ranges of Texas or, most beautiful of all perhaps, out under the great stars of the Mojave Desert with scent of sage and sand in my nostrils, and time and space illimitable things.

There have been the flowered nights of England, the heathered ones of Scotland, the moistured ones of Ireland; breathing the salt wind of Brittany or the thin, rock-scented air of the Pyrénées. Nights spent waiting for the dawn to encarnadine the snow peak of Popocatépetl or bring back to the waters of Crater Lake their deep blueness which is beyond that of heaven. Nights stumbling in darkness through the Ozarks or the woods of northern Ontario; perfumed, phosphorescent nights of Waikiki Beach, pine-scented nights of Quebec, salt-scented nights of British Columbia; nights of sun in summer-flowered Alaska and nights of driving rain in the gray-green Queen Charlotte Islands. So many nights with the sound of water running through them: salt and fresh, swift and still, clear and brackish.

So many nights with "the hills, rock-ribbed and ancient as the sun" keeping watch close by brown slopes of dark-earthed farmland. And now this night, with the Cocoosh Range at my shoulder and at my feet the sweet-voiced waters of a tiny river that is celebrated in neither song nor legend, but is known only to the very few who have gone this way. Yet, with most of the earth a traveled path behind me, it is here that I have found myself at last. It is here that I could stay for the rest of my life and, writing thousands of words each day, never exhaust the beauties and delights of these unstoried hills and streams.

Now "the night's silence, like a deep lamp, is burning with the light of the milky way," and the noise and hurry of the day have slipped down like a discarded garment. I am flung out upon this world with the lights of other worlds around me. It is simple now to see the universe clear and whole and not to be dismayed by it. It was once a great mass of diffused matter whirling gigantically in space, and who knows what it will be in the eons of tomorrow? But now it is plain and understood, with the heart if not with the mind, and the space and timelessness of it are like a healing salve upon the burns received on this hot and hurried earth.

When I go to the village, or worse still, to the nearest large town, I feel as though the words of the world poured down on me like hail. Words, words, millions of words like a great torrent that cannot be diverted or stayed. I remark, uninspiredly, that it is a nice morning and at once I am drenched with statistics on the past, present and future of the weather, complaints or adulation concerning the climate of this particular region and prophecies concerning the moisture or aridity of several months to come. I feel as though I were going down for the third time with no help in sight. That is the way I always feel when some stray observation of mine takes the stopper out of the jar, and words spill around me like water. But not like water either. They have not its music, its rhythmical flow, and it is only seldom that they seem to be making for any particular destination. No savage mountain torrent I have ever heard could equal the harshness of a spoken word. The fiercest ocean storm is a song compared to the sentences of argument, expostulation and slander that sow discord in almost any gathering of human beings.

We shall never understand one another until we reduce the language to seven words.

Words are meant to be the ties of communication, but now they have become the barriers of misunderstanding. We have forgotten the meaning of so many and we use even those we know so indiscriminately that the power is taken out of them, and they are only hollow shells which sound when struck but contain nothing of any value. We are seldom silent long enough to find the right word for that which we wish to say. Always there is just one word, one only, that will have the exact, delicate shade of meaning which we desire. But we cannot be bothered to look for such a word and afterward we wonder why we are misunderstood. Through custom and superstition certain words and phrases have worn grooves in our minds into which our thoughts automatically slide and which lead to the same emotions each time. This is the secret of propaganda. Those who wish to sway people know that they can always do so by the right catchword repeated often enough. I believe it was Chief Justice Holmes who said that such a catchword could put civilization back a hundred years. If totalitarian propaganda could have its way, civilization would be wiped out altogether.

So, it seems to me, we should watch our words more carefully than ever before and ask ourselves the real meaning of each one before we use it. If we could only realize the power and wealth and beauty of words, we would treasure them like jewels, bringing them out one by one to adorn the lovely garments of silence. If ever you consider yourself to be ill-treated, think how silence has been maligned. A man is silent; he is promptly called morose, odd, unsocial. Speech stops in a gathering — although usually no angels are going over the house — and immediately minds and faces are twisted in agony with the effort to start it again. That there should be a cessation of sound is one of the "sins" that society has marked as unpardonable. Medals are awarded to orators, but those who say nothing — perhaps more effectively — are given only black looks.

Yet there is such communion in silence. It is known to love and to deep friendship and it could be known to all of us if we would only let it be. How can we ever hope to give any good word to our neighbors or to humanity if we have no well of silence from which to draw the deep, cool waters of inspiration and refreshment? We pour out speech until our phrases rattle with emptiness — and what have we said? When I think of the years of my life that have been wasted in vapid conversation, I am ashamed. With a few exceptions I know now that any wisdom I have has come to me from slow reading and from solitude.

The written word usually has been considered and weighed before being put down on paper; it has been nurtured in silence and contemplation. But the spoken word jumps out of our mouths like Judy out of a box and generally with as little sense behind the gabbling. Speech was meant to be the communication of thoughts; now it is more often used to conceal them. So with Dionysius the Elder I say: "Let thy speech be better than silence, or be silent." It is as well for his peace of mind that he has been spared the torrent of words that has flowed on this earth since he left it in 367 B.C. We too know, bitterly, the truth of that saying which antedated his life: "For we must look about under every stone, lest an orator bite us."

The forest is still dark with night when I throw off the blanket of sleep and rouse thoroughly by plunging my head in the pool which has the gray-silver light of the waning moon on it. But soon it is reflecting the red flame of my fire, and the two remaining Dolly Vardens are sizzling succulently in the pan. While the corncakes are heating and the coffee water boiling (coffee is my weakness, but I have taken many trips on fireweed or Labrador tea and found those beverages as enjoyable as the journey), I pick black caps, blueberries and a few black currants for zest. Soon both meal and packing are finished and I am on the rough way to Serpentine canyon. I have to scramble over rocks, wade where I cannot climb and frequently take to the brush-covered banks.

I am still going up, for the river is four thousand feet higher at its source than at its outlet and there is a steep gradient all the way, although it is barely noticeable when following this part of the stream bed. There is a blazed trail where I am going, part of Placer Pike, but it is so faint and overgrown that I can make better time along the water's edge. On my first trip up here I followed it, as it crossed and recrossed the river, and found old sluice boxes put together with wooden nails and so rotten with age and moisture that you could poke a finger in them anywhere.

The sun is just over the mountains when I reach Serpentine canyon, but the gorge itself is still in darkness. The green stone and the green trees make it a place of wonder. The river bed is as smooth as though it had been hollowed by human hands. For fifty feet the walls are straight and high, with the river foaming through the entrance in a small waterfall and then subsiding into strong, deep quiet. The walls are rocky, with scant vegetation, but before and after the canyon the underbrush comes down to the water's edge again and the trees slope gradually away toward the mountains. Looking down into the water is like gazing into a cool, green cavern of polished stone belonging to some river nymph. The current is powerful but smooth, and the water so clear that it is possible to see everything below in minutest detail. When the sun shines down into the canyon, it is a corridor of green and golden beauty.

I am almost on the edge of the slates now and not far from where the river branches. The larger and longer branch tears down through the wild country of the Endahwin Range where mountains of granite have not been worn away by erosion as have those of the Cocoosh chain. I have followed both forks, and among the great moments of my life are those when I drank from the mountain springs which are the parents of the Wren.

So that is the course of this one small mountain river, not ancient in history as the Nile and the Euphrates, yet having its place and its story — more of a story than I or anyone shall ever learn. But the birds and the trees know some of it, the fishes more and the mountains most of all.

Just below Serpentine canyon a branch of Placer Pike runs toward Ipo mountain, joining the main trail at a point on Rue mountain near the by-path of Chert Lake. Bill and I have come through here several times with our axes and brush-hooks, but each summer finds the underbrush crowding the path, and windfalls everywhere. A belt of green timber runs through for some little distance; an oasis between two deserts left by fire. There is an early morning coolness on it now and in the open glades dew still iridesces on leaf and forest bloom. Vine maple, red alder, Hooker's willow, devil's club and salmonberry brush tangle beside the trail, but at the beginning the way is fairly clear and the slope gentle.

When the sound of the river has faded into nothingness, the silence is absolute except for the lisping syllables of the winter wren and the noise of my own progress. The forest flowers of other trails have been joined by the white Ipo on this, its namesake mountains. Silver-green rattlesnake plantain has taken the place of prince's pine which it so much resembles, and the holly-like leaves and blue berries of tall Oregon grape show everywhere. This member of the barberry family is, strangely enough, confined to the mountain slopes in this district, whereas its cousin *Berberis nervosa* grows in the lower valleys.

With berries ripening all around — for this is also the home of the blue currant with its pendulous raceme of blue berries and of the swamp gooseberry — I am not surprised to see that the bears have been here before me, for in the days of summer and early fall it is quite the usual thing to find half the fruit gone from a clump of bushes and to see a compact black form amble out serenely with several smug glances flung back over a furry shoulder. For these are the small black bears, the "clowns of the woods." Usually they are four to five feet long and about thirty inches high, but they are very solid and weigh around three hundred pounds. A close view shows that their fur has a brownish cast and their faces have a decidedly more amiable expression than those of their grizzly cousins who occasionally drift over from the farther mountains of this range.

The little black bears and I have never quarreled, even when the fruit was sweetest. We stick to our own patches or content ourselves with what is left. I scold them for the unseemly way in which they trample down the bushes just in order to make matters easier for themselves, and they have something to say about the scandalous amount of fruit I seem to need for my preserving kettles. I have yet to see one of them in a bad temper, although I know they can be — especially in the spring. But usually they have a glint of the eye and a comical twist of the head as they roll along with their naval gait or jump from stone to stone of the river banks. One youngster has been frisking around the Teal all summer. He has, I feel, so recently escaped from the nursery that he is trying to make the most of every moment in this big world of delicious sniffs and tidbits.

I am glad of the slacks pulled on over my shorts and of the long sleeves of my light wool shirt as I wrestle with devil's club and salmonberry brush in my upward climb. But soon the former grows scarcer, more black willows begin to appear and the ranks of Douglas fir, grand fir, Sitka spruce and western birch are considerably thinned. All of this country has been burned over — no primeval forest is left here now — but the particular strip that I am following has escaped the fires of more recent times and so boasts many coniferous trees that must be three hundred to four hundred years old or more. But now I begin to leave the big timber and familiar trunks behind me and to see the stranger bark, leaf and needles of western white pine — often called "silver pine" and with good reason — mountain birch, amabilis fir (that lovely tree!), yellow cypress and yew. The last-named is never found in quantity here and when it does appear, singly or in small groups, it shows a gnarled and stunted form.

Sometimes the branchlets that drop down from the sides make it look like a needled weeping willow; sometimes it is bent into a complete bow — reminding one that its wood has been used for that purpose for centuries. The coral-red berries, beloved by the birds, are not yet ripe, but those of the serviceberry bushes (everything is so much later here) should delight the Canada jays and the redstarts. Western teaberry and blue elderberries show at intervals, and the red stems of western dogwood stand out warmly against the surrounding green. Blue huckleberries bob up in sunny clearings and where the rock slides begin, blueberries are plentiful.

This is where I leave Placer Pike to angle around the mountain while I begin the hard, perspiring climb to the summit of Ipo. A creek bed running from the heights must be my trail; the lesser of two evils, for trying to cut a way through the underbrush would be worse than climbing over the big boulders of the channel. Windfalls are flung everywhere upon the ground for when a tree crashes on the higher slopes, it gains considerable momentum on its journey down and snaps off many others in its course. Roots, branches, trunks, rotting logs with club moss covering many of them, deep gullies and big rockslides are each a trap for the heedless foot, and progress becomes a wavering, uncertain thing of sweat and puff and fly bite.

I am glad of my light pack as the angle of ascent increases and the day becomes warmer. Douglas fir has been left behind now, while western hemlock is giving way to its mountain cousin. A few Rocky Mountain juniper and Sitka alder appear, with aspen and black cottonwood still showing but in smaller form. All the timber is smaller now, and tall, bare trunks have been replaced by low, numerous branches. Little colonies of rattlesnake plantain inhabit mossy log and boulder, and the sticky, pinkish pine drop nods its flowers from decaying vegetation. Blinks are here and the lovely parsley fern whose Latin name, *Cryptogramma acrostitchoides*, should delight all crossword puzzle fans. The small cranberry shows red fruit against green moss and makes me think of its tall cousin — so like a snowball bush when in bloom — which will be forming scarlet fruit at lower altitudes. By a steep bluff the mountain bilberry — more like the delicious eastern blueberry than any other I have found here — shows glossy blackness, but it will not be at its juicy best until September.

The bluff is a steep, stiff climb and when I reach the top I throw myself and my pack down on the ground near a clump of beech fern and lie there to breathe deeply and to rest. When I sit up and look around, I see one of the many rewards of this hard trail: green meadows with a tiny creek ambling through them and flowers flung across like the streamers of northern lights. The slope levels out here and I can look through the sparse timber, as through green-framed windows, to mountains on either side and far below the green valley of the Wren surrounded by the dark remains of fire. The sun beats hotly down on this high place and the air, at six thousand feet, is like clear golden wine. Blue-eyed grass and knotweed wave across the meadows and mountain phlox sways in the soft breeze. Blue lupine and mountain marigold surround a pool of melted snow where deer, bear, cougar and coyote tracks are clearly visible in the soft, damp earth. Rose spirea outlines the meadow borders, and the evergreen leaves of Labrador tea (the drink made from them is really delicious!) reveal their rusty undersides as the wind stirs them. Waist-high shrubs of white rhododendron show here and there — with a Hepburn's rosy finch perched on one of them — but their spring of ivory flowers like cherry blossoms — and smelling of bitter almonds — is over and now they wait in green retirement beside their colorful neighbors.

As though all this were not enough of beauty and delight, a silver waterfall sprays down from the peak of Ipo — two thousand feet above — to form the little stream that meanders through the iridescent grasses and to make a shimmering background for this lovely scene of the high solitudes. Mist maidens — as white as the veil that they embroider — are appliquéd upon the lace of maidenhair and the velvet of moss. The white-flowered bog orchid lifts its tall head not far away, and like a sunrise cloud, the small pink flowers of the mountain bleeding-heart rise above the light green of their soft and feathery leaves. The clear note of Townsend's solitaire sounds distantly, and a flock of mountain chickadees flutters down to whisper in the underbrush.

I feel that delirious sense of delight, which always comes at such moments, welling up inside me. It simply *is* and I *am* — and that is enough. There is prayer in it and thanksgiving; there is joy, humility, a touch of sadness and the very core of peace. I am alive in this world and the next and in all the world of space. Tree, flower and bird are my blood brothers and the golden clock of time has stopped so that I may listen to the swift beating of my many lives. Now I know why there is prayer: that there may be thanks given for all of this to the one Spirit who never fails to understand.

But there is a canker in Eden. It is the many and malicious mosquitoes that find these marshy meadows a perfect breeding place and inhabit them in swarms. If it were not for them I might stay and have lunch here, but after all it is only eleven and surely I can make the last two thousand feet of Ipo in a couple of hours. I must follow a dry creek bed again, but there will not be so many windfalls now for the timber has thinned greatly and what trees there are grow to no height. The underbrush lessens also as I resume my boulder-clambering, but rockslides increase and the stony sides of the mountain are pitted with gullies and great holes that seem to have been gouged out by some giant hand.

Englemann spruce (a beautiful tree when in solid stands) has added its pungent odor to the spice of white pine, with the strong, sharp scent of the blue-green alpine fir overriding them both. A few lodgepole pine and amabilis fir are here also, and mountain alders show quite densely beside the stream bed I am following. As I climb higher, the stunted forms of aspen and mountain birch are interspersed with Barclay's and low willow — which are only small shrubs here — and the gnarled dwarf junipers display their silver-bloomed dark fruit. But loveliest of all is the mountain ash, with brilliant red berries like jewels among its branches. That beautiful rowan tree — ivory-flowered in spring and early summer, rubied in fall — a twig of which was for centuries considered by Europeans to be a sure protection against all evil spirits.

If there were ever any evil spirits here, the rowan has touched them and they have fled — down and down the slopes and into the ugly, clustered buildings that spring like some noisome growth from asphalt and from steel. But the groundhog evidently has no faith in omens, for I can hear his shrill whistle warning mountain goat and white-tailed ptarmigan that danger is approaching. As I arrive at the summit — dripping with perspiration, even in this cooler mountain air, and completely winded from dodging great willow and alder thickets and the deep snowdrifts that lie in shady hollows — a Clarke's crow streaks across in front of me and then his harsh voice expostulates from somewhere out of sight. The lovely yellow fireweed has been lighting my way as I climbed, but now other light — white, rose, yellow and blue — shines into my eyes from the borders of a tiny alpine lake which the sun has turned into a dazzling jewel in a setting of gray stone carved by the elements and tinted softly with the hues of mountain flowers.

It is almost an incongruous thing, this untroubled shining water where every tree has been bent double by the fierce, cold storms that sweep across these heights, and every flower clings closely to the weathered soil or hides in crevices so that it will not be blown out into vast space. Everything here speaks of struggle and of resolute endurance — even the delicate blue gentian patching the dark ground or the pale yellow beard-tongue like thin sunlight against gray stone. Snow has surged down upon this peak in white fury, wind has howled like a thousand banshees across its length and breadth, rain has tattered and depleted it and clouds have wrapped it in clammy chill for days and nights together. The forked, white tongue of lightning has licked earth and stone, striking with venom at a crouching tree. Thunder has gone, roaring with anger, through these passes, and the mountains have tossed the sound one to another like a great, dark ball before they allowed it to roll down into the valleys and be still.

But there have been days like this day: warmed by sun and with the wind a bright, familiar thing. Days of clear blue sky with river and forest spread out below in green, untroubled beauty. Dawns when the sun rose from beyond the world's blue edge like heaven's gold, and small, rosy clouds danced to the music of the horned lark above Ipo's lake and flowers. Nights when the stars seemed no higher than the reach of my hand as they hung down on invisible chains to light the great hall of earth. Nights like a dark river lit by fireflies, flowing back into the primeval past and forward into the mysterious future.

I have lain awake whole nights through, here on Ipo and on other mountains higher, with the sharp, thin air pricking my face and creeping up from the hard ground to dilute the warmth of my sleeping bag. But that was not the reason for my wakefulness. I did not sleep because I could not bear to miss one moment of this high beauty; this tryst with far-traveled sky and new, keen air; this rendezvous with life. The very altitude that slows the steps and accelerates the heart also brings a certain calm clarity to the mind that I have never known so fully in any other place. The lessening of the heavier oxygen of lower lands tunes each sense into higher perceptivity at the same time that it lays a light, soporific veil across the mind and relaxes the swift tension between brain and muscle. The first slight dizziness passes, to be replaced by such calm exultation that one's thoughts can walk quietly among the stars with truth, the fretted earth just an illusion of the body and only the unseen actual and near.

I would like to have another night such as this on Ipo, only there are many miles of mountain forest between here and home where my growing things are parching under the hot August sun. But there is luncheon at least — cold corncakes, hot coffee in a thermos and half a pail of black caps that have survived the journey well — beside the tiny lake with alpine spiraea, and moss campion forming my tablecloth of rose-purple and white and a great golden eagle flaring across the deep blue sky with the sunlight glinting on his wings. The fluffy white flowers of hare's tail wave beside the water and the mountain asters peer out at me from crevices where it seems impossible that any life could exist. Mountain phacelia spreads its purple blossoms along the ground in joyous contrast to the stern, gray rocks that form its backdrop. The reddish blooms and evergreen leaves of mountain lover blossoming late this year seem to be pushing back the still unmelted snow of sheltered places, mingling with the blue-purple flowers of Menzie's beard-tongue to make a picture, silhouetted against shining white, which can never be forgotten.

But perhaps it is the red and white heathers—no true heather, really—which are the loveliest of all. Their bell flowers and needle leaves are bright against lichened boulders, and I find my ears straining to catch those soft chimes that surely must be sounding. The yellow dogtooth violet—or glacier lily as it is more beautifully named—wafts its fragrance across my face and mingles it with the clean, dry wind. Pear-leaf and sedge intermingle beside that pool of peace which is an alpine lake. Pipit and rosy finch have appeared and disappeared while I was eating and, as I lie back against the rocks to savor my coffee and this perfect hour, a raven is silhouetted darkly against the delphinium-blue sky. But he says nothing to me of "Nevermore."

On the northern slope of Ipo a gully filled with snow reaches down almost three thousand feet to the timbered and meadowed lands which run northwest toward Rue mountain and Chert Lake. That snow, only about three or four feet deep at most and still hard below its melting surface, solves my problem of how to get down the mountain quickly. It is clear of obstruction almost all the way and I slide, plunge, slither, sink and skid down its entire length, shouting as I go. What the bald eagle thinks of this performance I do not know — or the cliff swallows, which make such a shocked and startled swerve away from my boisterous descent. But I am very happy — even when I arrive breathless at the bottom to find myself soaked through with snow and perspiration and to feel the sharp knifeblade of the mountain wind slitting my clothes. A flock of pipits looks at me and twitters: "Serves you right!"

But trying to find the easiest way through meadow and woodland or cutting a path through matted alder, maple and willow leaves me no opportunity to feel really cold. I nod to the goldenrod buds which are beginning to form and say "hello" to the rain orchids and mountain valerian. In wet places I look eagerly for elephant trunk and on dry slopes for its lousewort cousin.

Now I am walking again where fingers of fire have reached into this green land and left only skeletons behind with purple willowweed to decorate the graves. I cross this stretch as quickly as I can for I am sick at heart whenever I see such needless death where life was once so urgent and so sweet. Green timber comes again finally and then a bluff with water cascading over rocks green with moss and bright with the familiar flowers of lower altitudes: miner's lettuce, pipsissewa, bedstraw and twinflower. Here the firefighters camped in those past days of fury and here I shall camp tonight with a ruby-crowned kinglet and a hermit thrush for company. No, not quite, but in a little clearing nearby where I can see the stars. There I build my fire and, my frugal supper over — I had expected to have time to climb the trail to Chert Lake on Rue and catch some fish — lie beside it in my sleeping bag and relax in tired content.

The tangy perfume of earth is close and sharp in my nostrils; a cool, tree-scented wind passes across my face and somewhere in the distance two coyotes salute the stars. I feel boneless and fluid and so utterly relaxed that I seem to be flowing along the ground rather than lying upon it. Sometime in the very early morning I awaken for a few moments to find a silver wedge of moon, worn thin with age, slanting down on me and illuminating my clearing like a dawn.

Then — it *is* dawn, with winter wren and Audubon's warbler telling me so dulcetly. A squirrel emphasizes it — not so dulcetly — and a chipmunk scampers off as I sit up and look around me. Soon I am walking along Placer Pike once more — it is only a few steps away from the rock bluff — and looking for the turnoff to Chert Lake, although I shall not have time to follow it. There is a mailbox there, nailed to a hemlock, for several prospectors once lived up on Rue and whoever went through left mail and supplies for them. Rue is two thousand feet lower than Ipo, but Chert Lake is larger than the tiny alpine lake — called Carum after the Latin name for Ipo — on the latter and about half a mile long by one-sixteenth mile wide. There is a creek at one end and it is said that a great deal of gold has been taken out of this area.

Of course all prospectors, like all fishermen, have their tales, each one a little longer and a little wilder than the last. I know two, over seventy, who can do beautiful embroidery, but that only makes their yarns more entertaining. I have no intention of writing a guidebook or a history of this country — I shall leave that to more methodical heads than mine — and so I am delighted to hear the story of the bear cub in the tree, the cougar on the rock and sagas of Indian days. The two ancients who tell them could take me up the mountains and lose me with no trouble at all and even if I managed to keep going in the right direction they could leave me so far behind that they would be cooking their second meal when I arrived panting at the door. Their eyes are clear, their backs only a little bowed and if their hearing is fading a trifle, their philosophy is still sound.

Now I am walking, on a slight downward slope, along the ridge that connects Rue and Cougar mountains. I have windows on the world again and every now and then these openings framed in evergreen show me the mountains of the Endahwin Range spread out to the westward, the snow of the high peaks like gleaming alabaster in the sunlight. Here are the true riches of the earth and I pity those who have never known how wealthy one can be without a penny in the pocket. It is wealth that no one can ever steal and no inflation can depreciate. Yet I would not try to convince anyone that this life of mine would be the life for him.

Such things are like true friendship; when you are ready for them they will come to you. It is necessary also to be utterly convinced that they *are* yours, for otherwise you will not be able to withstand the criticism and sneers of those who think that their way is the only way and all others utterly mad. It must be all or nothing, for if you begin to sway to and fro in the wind of censure it would be far wiser to return to the approbation of your neighbors, for you will be able to do no good either to yourself or to others. This is true of any sort of life. If you do not live it thoroughly it would be better, I think, if you did not live it at all — although I realize that such a drastic course would probably depopulate the earth.

The dictionary defines life as "the active principle." *Active*, please observe: doing something about it, not just allowing ourselves to be pushed around this way and that without an idea of where we, as entities, are going or any clear and independent effort to arrive at our destination even if we know what it should be. Today we decide that such and such a course is the one for us to take, but our neighbor says: "If you do that then the So-and-So's will never invite you to dinner again and so you will lose both prestige and money."

So we, having so little in ourselves that we must always court the approval of others, start on another tack and soon it all ceases to matter, for we become unable to distinguish truth from falsehood, but resemble a sailboat becalmed in a windless gray dawn, suspended between sky and water and at the mercy of any least puff of wind. I, with Marcus Aurelius, "have often wondered how it is that every man loves himself more than all the rest of man, but yet sets less value on his own opinion of himself than on the opinions of others."

When I start down the steep path from the crest of Cougar to the Wren, my berry pails are almost full of black caps, blueberries and elderberries and I wonder just where I can put the black currants which were my alleged reason for this trip. I seriously consider tying my jacket together, lining it with leaves and using it for an emergency berry bag. If I could only be sure that I would not arrive home with fruit juice. Well, tomorrow is another day — which always reminds me of a neighbor woman who tried to explain to me just why her new house, in which she had lived for several days, was no nearer to being settled than when she had first moved in: "Monday", she said, "I had to do the washing and Tuesday the stove broke down and Wednesday some people came in and yesterday," she paused and wrinkled her forehead in thought, then beamed triumphantly at me, "well, yesterday was yesterday!"

So tomorrow is tomorrow and I can go up to the big currant patches of the Wren, not far from my cabin, and fill my pails again.

The sun has gone down behind Home Wood as I pull myself across the river; the rocks are gray and the waters dark. It is that lovely time of twilight when the earth seems to be settling down between cool, green sheets after the warmth and activity of the day. The scent of mignonette and nicotiana drifts across my garden and an acraea moth wings idly over the delphinium. A hummingbird clearwing is feverishly dipping from flower to flower as though it must equal, in an hour or so, the work of its daylight competitors. A bee has gone peacefully asleep in a California poppy while others cling to the small blue flowers of the cynoglossum which they love so well. Maestro calls a greeting and drowsy twitterings come from the edge of the forest as the last golden light fades over Fireweed.

I stop and look around and know that I can never have enough of looking. As in a great love, each reunion is as though it were the first meeting. The little cabin, appearing to have pushed up through the brown earth with the trees and flowers by which it is surrounded, nestles its green roof against the darker green of the conifers in calm prelude to sleep. There are familiar faces everywhere and once again my heart and eyes are filled with the beauty and delight of this, my home. The door opens easily under my hand.

7

Now
in September

Strata jacent passim sua quaeque sub arboe poma.
(The apples lie scattered everywhere, each under its
*   tree.)*

VIRGIL

September is that month between when "time hangs goldenly on now" and each day is like the slow caress of a friend reluctant to depart. My summer work outside is over, except for watering, and my work of autumn has not yet begun. Only one fruit, the silver-blue elderberry, has yet to ripen and in this ninth month its hour comes. So, too, does mine to gather it, to bring it home in pails and make it into delicious jelly or wine-dark syrup to be poured over my griddlecakes on frosty mornings.

But the day on which I go elderberry picking has no thought of winter. The rivers are at their lowest and softest and when I wade across the Teal the water comes only to my knees, although it has the mountain chill of the nights of early fall. The sun is at noon, glinting from falls and rapid and striking down even into the dark depths of Dubh Glas. It shines on boulders and gravel laid bare on either side of the stream and touches the dusky-pink of chert, the pale green of serpentine and the lustrous darkness of black slate to jewel-like color. A faint stirring of the air brings the scent of evergreen and forest earth and bracken, telling me that the woods of Main Street and Timber Trail will be cool and fragrant on this warm afternoon.

Everything is so green along Main Street now. The leaves of the tall black cottonwood, the trembling aspen and the Hooker's willow with its red-brown bark have not yet begun to turn clear golden or yellow-brown or those of the straight-trunked red alder to fall while still colored with summer. The ancestors of these trees were growing on the earth during its first ages. Willows and poplars are among the earliest tree forms of the Lower Cretaceous period on this continent, while remains of alders have been found in Eocene rocks of the Tertiary era. The black cottonwood is often referred to here as "silver poplar," a name one can understand when the wind blows and exposes the silvery undersides of the dark green leaves, making the tree look as though it were white-flowered.

The Indians found a use for nearly all the trees of this district. The tender inner sap bark of western hemlock and aspen constituted food; root and branch of Sitka spruce were woven into baskets; the gum of grand fir was turned into ointment; the bark of red cedar transmuted into clothes and the trunk fashioned into canoes. The western birch also was used in canoe-making, both on this continent and in Britain where those boats go back to earliest days. Oddly enough, remains of the early British birch canoes were found in the gravel of the Clyde banks where the great ships of peace and war go out today. As to the use made of birch twigs, well, the children of early settlers (on whom the rod was *not* spared) should certainly know all about that! The wood of the western yew was taken not only for bows, but for paddles, halibut hooks and whenever strength and durability were the chief requisites. The orange-sweet sap of the lodgepole pine was considered to be a great delicacy by the natives, while that of the red alder — so called because its sap turns a dull crimson on exposure to air — was a favorite dye. The weather-resistant woods of yellow cypress and red cedar were prized in building, while maple, alder, willow, cherry, serviceberry and apple took their turn at being fashioned into arrow shafts, boxes, cutlery, furniture and other articles.

A use was found for almost every growing thing — uses that we, who pride ourselves on our ingenuity and make-do spirit, have neglected and ignored. Many of my teas — ginger, mint, camomile, sage, Labrador, fireweed, dandelion root, violet, elderflower and clover — come from the wilderness now, while salads of mustard, dandelion, sorrel, wild onion, plantain, lamb's quarters, shepherd's-purse and many other wild young shoots and sprouts are no novelty. Sourdough — yeast, flour and water mixed and put away in a crock until it has a very nasty smell indeed — is my steadfast friend and one whose friendship grows better year by year. The more I use it for bread and biscuits and flapjacks the whiter and sweeter it becomes, although mine is only a fledgling compared to the twenty-year vintages of some human "sourdoughs" I know.

Soup, for me, has changed from something poured out of a can into a much more delicious something simmered for hours in a pot, although finding the meat for it — for those who, unlike

myself, hunt with a gun instead of a camera — can mean leaping from crag to crag of these perpendicular mountains taking pot-shots at deer and goat. But in the end there is really soup: succulent, body-warming, soul-satisfying soup. Potato with a hint of carraway, cabbage with a touch of coriander, meat broth with a flicker of sage. Spices — except the wild or home-grown variety — are on my luxury list, but when I can obtain the "civilized" kind I use them freely: cinnamon, nutmeg or mace with apple, whole cloves with cabbage, cayenne with fruits and many other combinations. So many intricacies of flavor and nourishment that our grandparents employed have passed out of our knowledge, but the lean days may come again and send us out into the fields in search of health and savory delight. We shall never find Mother Nature's cupboard bare.

Creeping forest plants and moss are under my feet now and evergreens —not so large as those that the lumberjacks have taken, but still large enough — stretch up toward the deep blue sky above me,

> *Ivies spring better of their owne accord,*
> *Unwanted plots much fairer trees afford.*
> *Birds by no art much sweeter notes record.*

A winter wren remains confidingly on a nearby stump as I walk past, and I catch a swift black and white glimpse of a tree swallow silhouetted against blue sky. Timber Trail, where the blue elderberries are, branches west from Main Street to parallel Village Road at a lower level. But the twenty clear miles it ran formerly have now been cut to three by the machinations of water and of rock. In its days of gold and glory it was a wagon road used to freight supplies from the village — then a thriving community of six hundred souls — to the various placer diggings. After the coming of steel, it was still used as a supply road when the railroad was closed down by heavy slides, but now only the pole cutters, Bill and I know it well.

The forest is cool and shadowy, with light shafting through the trees and every now and then a lovely sun-shot vista of the path opening up ahead. The purple flowers of hedge nettle are bloom-ing and the Douglas aster has come into its own royal beauty. In the open, drier clearings pearly everlasting — whose other name of "moonshine" is even more alluring — hawkweed and golden-rod mingle their white and yellow with the ivory and purple of woolly and Canada thistle. The former is a surprise to me as it usually frequents drier and more easterly latitudes. Here is a true and simple picture of September done in her favorite colors.

This district is supposed to be deficient in wildflowers, but where the idea originated from I cannot imagine. It is true that many plants grow singly or in small groups and are not easy to discover, but I have been able to identify over two hundred varieties — without going down to the village where flora is much more abundant — although some of them have been represented by only a single flower. It is the same with the birds: many families are represented, but there may be only pairs or small groups of each, and many times I have encountered only a single specimen. But the opening of the opera season brings wren, thrush, robin, grosbeak, swallow, swift, blackbird, warbler, finch, jay, ouzel, sparrow, junco and many, many others to take part in the proceedings or give catcalls from the gallery. Some of them are year-round residents of my valley, but for Townsend's solitaire and other kindred spirits it is necessary to go up into the mountains.

Others are glimpsed only in migrations, and some that are observed one year may not be seen again for three or four. One autumn I had just finished sowing grass seed when a flock of pipits appeared from the high hills and proceeded to have a hearty and — very obviously — enjoyable meal. Apparently they passed the good word along, for no sooner had I repaired the damages than an even larger number of plump little pine siskins dropped out of the treetops to sample the table d'hôte — and I did not see either bird near the cabin for the next three years. Neither did I see much results from my grass seed, but the gain was more than worth the loss,

> *In nature's infinite book of secrecy*
> *A little I can read. . . .*

but it is difficult for me, even with the best will in the world, to know all my singing and flowering neighbors. Many of them are very shy and several are extremely reticent where my acquaintance is concerned. They value friendship as it should be valued and offer it only after I have shown myself to be worthy of their trust.

I have sat or lain patiently for hours in the forest, on hillsides and by creeks and rivers waiting for even a glimpse of a feathered resident or visitor. I have followed goat trails to high mountain flowers and splashed through streams and swamps looking for the blossoms of low places. I have done my best to preserve a good relationship, and I have been rewarded past any hope or dream. Slowly, but very certainly, I have been taken into the confidence of these neighbors, and each year has brought me more of wonder and delight. Naturally they are not all full of beaming sweetness nor would I wish them to be.

There are those who add the salt and spice and who keep me shaking my head over their all-too-human traits. I shall, I feel, never be a bosom friend of the deer fly or "no-see-um" nor can I imagine myself taking a companionable stroll through the woods with a grizzly or a cougar. Nevertheless, I have considerable respect for these ladies and gentlemen and, so far, the two last-mentioned have shown the same for me.

To watch the seedpods of the mesembryanthemum open out into five-pointed stars (the "star of destiny," so revered by gipsy fortunetellers) when placed in water or discover that one of our Indian wars was caused by white settlers encroaching on the camas meadows of the Nez Percés — how much more interesting that is than to listen to John Jones tell the same dull joke for the fiftieth time or to Mrs. Jones' complaints of the younger generation! In a few days or weeks — or even hours! — I can empty many human minds, but if I were to live here for the rest of my life I could never exhaust the possibilities of flower and fruit and tree and stone.

O! mickle is the powerful grace that lies
In herbs, plants, stones, and their true qualities. . . .

Every day I find something I have not seen before: something that may send me delving into botany, geology, ornithology, dendrology, zoology, astronomy, chemistry or history — back, back to the very beginning of life on this planet. But although my own life has been more varied and gone further afield than most, I have found only a dozen or so souls who stimulated me as these wilderness companions of mine have done. Here is not "the glass of fashion and the mould of form"; no face and foliage aping the color and line of others, but a variety of individual shapes and shades which is a joy to the discoverer.

The monkshood I seek out in high places is like, yet unlike, the aconitum of my garden, while the wild bouvardia of dry ground differs enough from the gilia I have known to intrigue and captivate me. There is a charming Klamath legend, recorded by Doctor Coville and by Charles Francis Saunders, that in old times the doves drank only the nectar of the scarlet gilia of the Rockies and that is why it is still called "Oblsam bohnwas," "the drink-plant of the doves." The white flowers of the black nightshade appear at all times and places and keep me interestedly on the watch for them. The pimpernel has so many names — Johnny-go-to-bed-at-noon, poor man's weather glass, shepherd's warning — that I suspect a mysterious past in the Old World and am always trying to find out more about it. No fireside reminiscence can carry me back in memory as swiftly as the aromatic odor of yerba buena or the sight of its small mauve flowers. At once I am walking the steep, foggy streets of San Francisco again or watching the harbor lights from Telegraph Hill as I think back to the days before 1846 when that now-great metropolis bore the name of a little creeping plant.

Many rockslides have hurtled down from upper Fireweed since last I walked Timber Trail, and their deep gravel makes heavy going. Thimbleberries and a few red and blue huckleberries still show beside them with common plantain and rib grass wherever the sun shines. I have evidently disturbed a varied thrush at his fruit course and now he is perched up in a Sitka spruce with a decidedly disgruntled expression showing above his black tie. These Alaska robins are quite tame around here, especially in spring and fall when they are everywhere in flocks, and it is possible to take excellent photographs of them from as close as four feet. The ones who live near my cabin are very fond of the clothesline — as are the hummingbirds also, when they can bring themselves to alight anywhere — and will perch there contentedly for several minutes at a time, quite undisturbed by my comings and goings. The winter wrens, on the other hand, prefer the top of the woodsheds, and at intervals during late summer Mrs. robin will also sit there by the hour uttering the most doleful cheeps. On those occasions I suspect that Mr. robin has gone down to the village, in spite of his wife's protests, and will probably come home in the wee sma' hour flying in circles.

Know you why the robin's breast
Gleameth of a dusky red,
Like the luster 'mid the stars
Of the potent planet Mars?
'Tis – a monkish myth has said–
Owing to his cordial heart;
For, long since, he took the part
Of those hapless children, sent
Heavenward, for punishment;
And to quench the fierce desire
Bred in them by ruthless fire,
Brought on tiny bill and wing
Water from some earthly spring.

Just beyond the largest rockslide a deer trail crosses my path, running down Fireweed toward the Teal. The white-tailed buck and his doe are becoming scarcer here owing to the small gray coyotes who have so increased their numbers in recent years. I have never seen a timber wolf in the vicinity, but I have heard their far voices in the night when I was camping out in the mountains. Immediately I was back in the Sangre de Cristo mountains of New Mexico, in the Coeur d'Alene district of Idaho or lying awake on a small island in Ontario's Temagami Lake where the cry of the pack would come across the midnight water like sharpened, savage chimes.

The coyote and the cougar, like the screech owl, apparently have never come across that admonition to be "seen and not heard." They reverse it very neatly, however, and the wild howl of the one and the chilling scream of the other are not uncommon sounds, although they seldom show themselves. But their tracks are familiar sights, especially those of an old coyote larger than the others who travels alone across and across my property and who has, I am sure, been near me as I walked home in darkness from a trip to the village or some other

ramble abroad. I have seen the eyes of the lynx then, too, following me at some distance in the underbrush as I moved along the
trail. He seems to have quite a fondness for such sleuthing, so I
judge him to be a rather curious fellow and perhaps not averse
to a bit of human companionship. The fact that he is quite easily
captured would seem to bear me out in this.

But if the mountain lion cares for two-footed companionship
he has not announced it to me, although I have seen his tracks
everywhere and followed many a trail that he had traveled not
long before me. Once I came face to face with him as I rounded a
ledge of rock, and he reminded me of nothing so much as the
Cheshire cat. One moment he was there and the next he had
dissolved silently into the landscape while an impression of him
seemed to linger on the mountain air. But he did *not* smile.

Nearly all the larger animals here are enemies of the deer, and
I wish that graceful creature could know that I am its friend.
Fisher, mink, marten, wolverine (and *he* never will be missed!)
and flying squirrel are becoming scarcer also thanks to the trapper, hunter and fisherman — while the beavers have made their
last stand at Beaver Lake, which is some distance from where I
have made mine. The fur of the wolverine is very valuable for
use in cold climates for it possesses the unique quality of never
frosting, but his thieving manners are deplorable and it is no
wonder that he has received the appellation of "glutton."

The gray and red squirrel, Oregon chipmunk, shrew, small
weasel, meadow and mule mouse do their best to make up in
numbers what they lack in size, with a few porcupines and
skunks to help matters along. In the Endahwin and Cocoosh
ranges I have found the trails of the mountain goat a great help
although often beyond my agility. While following one, I have
been amused to hear the shrill warning whistle of the groundhog,
who evidently thought I was doing my stalking with something
more lethal than a camera and binoculars. I can imagine the
annoyance of real hunters when his danger signal rang out and
the thankful quarry took flight! But if I am not annoyed on the
heights, I am down at my cabin by the occasional pack rat who
takes up his abode — very temporarily, I might say — in my attic
and by the deer and white-footed field mice who think that I am
the proprietor of the village store, although I have never noticed

Scotty

that they offered to pay for anything, which is something the pack rat always does.

I also object to the way these innocent-looking little rodents, with long tails and short ones, girdle my trees, eat my flowers and vegetables and devour my bulbs if I fail to put naphthalene around them. In the last pursuit as well as in the second one they are enthusiastically joined by the many chipmunks who delight in sitting up on my stumps with one eye on me and the other on the embryo grape hyacinth they are nibbling with gusto. I do not miss the lone bunny who arrived one morning, ate up a whole row of young cabbage and then disappeared forever, apparently. Nor would I shed a tear if every slug — giant Pacific, European or garden variety — vanished overnight. But I would certainly feel bereft without the red squirrels who slide down my roof or the pair of grays who chase each other over the garden with such verve and frolic that it is pure delight to watch them.

The squirrels are busy here this afternoon, running up and down the evergreens or pausing to sit on a branch and give their unsolicited opinion of the day in general and myself in particular. Not far ahead I hear the drumming of the ruffed grouse begin, first quite slowly and then accelerating in tempo until there is just a blur of sound. His wings were also a blur of motion when I caught him in the act on Placer Pike as he paraded along a hemlock log with ruff, tail and crest on beautiful display. His autumnal drumming has nothing to do with courting, but probably means that he is feeling as full of joy as I am.

A bear has evidently been through on Timber Trail this morning, for I can see where some of the blue berries of Oregon grape — a few that I missed! — have been picked and the plants trampled. The trail closes up here with small evergreens, ferns and snowberry bushes, the last named with its white fruit shining from the branches. As children we used to delight in the "pop" these gave when stepped on — and I can still never resist treading on at least one. Beyond this the trail opens out to run over a corduroy section which, in spring and late fall, is running with water. The light-red berry clusters of the coral honeysuckle glow beside it, and the dusky twins of alpine beauty show along the ground with the scarlet starflower fruit. Golden berries of the fairy bell swing beside the signal red of false solomon's seal and twisted-stalk, with the white globes of western dogwood gleaming against dark crimson leaves. The edible thistle — whose roots the Indians found to be such an excellent substitute for sugar — adds another brilliant touch and a stray sunflower supplements the sun. The valerian is still in bloom, its purple spotted fruit yet to come, beside the lovely blue mallow.

Now comes one of the prettiest parts of this autumn trail: a grove of evergreens where tall hemlocks and firs — saved by some miracle from the ax — still stand between their taller neighbors and huge cedar stumps of bygone years. It is like a great cathedral, with its straight tree-pillars and the westering sun penetrating a green bush tangle at the end as though it were shining through stained-glass windows.

> *. . . Storied windows richly dight*
> *Casting a dim religious light.*

The forest walls rise dark on either side and the sound of the river comes faintly, like the singing of an unseen choir. There is a feeling of immensity here; huge boulders, water-rounded or sharp from the erosion of Fireweed, are everywhere. It is not difficult to think back to the times when the Carboniferous rocks of this area were laid down by a submergence of seawater and twenty thousand feet of submarine deposits accumulated; to lava flows and reelevation and other marine incursions as the earth was twisted and wrung in the agony of that great birth.

When the oldest rocks of this district were formed, life was just beginning to come out of the waters onto the land — plants first and then animals — and now we can read that travelogue in the fossils of fern, moss, centipede and scorpion. Huge insects swarmed in and near the swamps, for all of life was in these low places while the uplands were still barren and without vitality. The frog represents today that Carboniferous yesterday, and of the era that followed, the Age of Reptiles, we have examples in the snake, turtle and crocodile. Even with the tropics in mind it is difficult to visualize the hothouse conditions under which they and other species — which today are found only in our museums — must have existed on the marshy plains and among the still flowerless trees and plants of the Mesozoic forests. The beginning of our bird and animal life was there also, but the few strange representatives would hardly have been noticed while the great dinosaurs and pterodactyls roamed the land and air.

For something like 80 million years this time of warmth and abundance lasted; then came cold and death, and at the end of several million more years new and sturdier flora and fauna emerged to enter into the Carnivore period or the Age of Mammals. Extreme volcanic activity took place then — 60 million years ago — as the great mountain ranges were thrown up and the outlines of new continents and oceans began to appear. The winter of the beginning of this Tertiary era was followed by another summer and that again was followed by the austere cold — with warmer intervals between — of the four Glacial Ages. Man-like things appeared during that time, although we have no absolutely accurate knowledge as to when the first true man developed.

So the Quatenary era began. The years moved on and on until at about the time Sargon, the Semitic barbarian, was conquering the cultured Sumerians and founding an empire, seed took root in what is now the soil of California and grew into that big tree under which I stood only a few years ago in Sequoia National Park. When Northmen (Russians) were engaged in wresting England from the Low Germans, a big redwood acquaintance of mine was a sturdy young sapling and when the Ottoman Turks were taking Constantinople, some Engelmann spruce I met in these mountains were enjoying childhood. When Bebber swept across the plains of India, the western hemlock to which my Teal cable is attached was taking youthful looks at life, while at the time of the Declaration of Independence my old friend, the Douglas fir, had seen over two hundred years of flood and forest fire.

Red cedar stumps which are around me now, logged in recent years, were mature trees when Columbus landed on this continent. Juniper, Sitka spruce, white pine and yellow cypress of these uplands have seen centuries come and go. Before Napoleon marched into Portugal, certain of my alpine and amabailis fir neighbors were healthy adolescents and when Britain and France began their struggle for America and India, some lodgepole pine and grand fir inhabitants were definitely out of rompers. Two specimens of Douglas fir that were picked up outside this district show that one tree — cut down in 1900 — was a seedling when Edward III ascended the throne of England, while the rings of the other proved the tree to be around three thousand years old, although with that one there was no way of telling its diameter.

Half a million years ago animals roamed these mountains that are now only a legend of a few teeth and bones found by some panning prospector or exposed by the weathering of an old cliff face. Dinosaurs were here and mastodons. The Columbian elephant came for only a short time, but the hairy mammoth with his long, shaggy brown hair and undercoat of thick wool was a resident for many thousands of years. The mule deer — whose descendants still inhabit these woods — sought shelter in the forests while the musk ox and broad-horned bison roamed the plains of Pleistocene times. But that yesterday of half a million years ago is no more alien to today than today will seem to those who pass over Timber Trail half a million years from now. I wish that I might be one of them, whoever they are and in whatever form.

No one could think of these things and not think also of the greatness and littleness of man. So much he has done in his thousands of years of life, so much he has left undone that might have been accomplished. The earth was his "and the fullness thereof." It is easy to become discouraged at the slowness of his progress, but when we place his life so far against even the 1.6 billion years of the world, as recorded in the rocks, it seems like such a flashing second that we stand amazed before his achievements. Yet that does not prevent us from being impatient with him to do more and more. So much of his brain power is not even being used, so many of the ideas born in that brain have not been translated into action. In one century, the sixth B.C., Greek philosophers, Hebrew prophets and teachers of India and China were opening up a new world to humanity, but now, in the twentieth century, many of the greatest truths they discovered and proclaimed are left to become dusty upon our shelves while we continue to practice the ways of barbarism.

Not many of us on this continent profess to be philosophers or prophets so we cannot be blamed if we fail in that area, but the majority of us do profess to be Christians and therein lies our greatest defeat. Christ told us, simply and beautifully, how life could and should be — yet how many of us have ever tried to carry out his gospel in its sublime entirety? We say that we believe in him, but that is only a word upon the lips and not a faith in the heart. If it were otherwise we would be trying to live as he lived so that we might make our world into the place of life and truth that he envisioned. If Christ were here now, even in this democracy, many people would feel that he should be either in an asylum or in a jail, while he would almost certainly be deported or interned in wartime for telling us to love our enemies. While he lived, he died not the one death of crucifixion but the thousand deaths of misunderstanding and intolerence — and it would be the same today. Yet I believe that one day we shall find that he was right and that the only way to obtain peace and decency and plenty for all is to follow his teachings. It is not too large a work for the least of us. In our own lives each one of us can practice kindness, understanding, truth. In this way we shall create a new nation and that nation will, in turn, help to create a new world.

Plato said: "Most of the social and political ills from which you suffer are under your control, given only the will and courage to change them. You can live in another and wiser fashion if you choose to think it out and work it out. You are not awake to your own power." "The will and courage": that is where most of us fail. Even if we believe, we are afraid to say so. We would rather, actually, be a replica of our neighbors than a pattern of that Jesus whom we profess to adore. He knew that when he said: "This people honoreth me with their lips, but their hearts are far from me. Howbeit in vain do they worship me, teaching for doctrines the commandments of men. For laying aside the commandment of God, ye hold the tradition of men, as the washing of pots and cups: and many other such like things ye do. And he said unto them: Full well ye reject the commandment of God, that ye may keep your own tradition." Twelve hundred years later Roger Bacon exclaimed: "Cease to be ruled by dogmas and authorities; look at the world!" Now we are indeed being forced to look at it and to look at it whole. Read what Christ says of nationalism and family life and then think back over the recent movement of ideas toward a larger viewpoint which will embrace not only our own family or nation, but all humanity. During wars we are urged to think not personally, but nationally; yet we shall have to think internationally in all things if we hope to survive. So, very slowly, the way of life which Christ proclaimed nearly two thousand years ago is beginning to obtain form and substance today. It will, I am convinced, follow this pattern more and more until, in the end, we find not only that truth which will make us free but that great happiness which Jesus knew and which we have denied ourselves so long.

On these walks and sitting in my little cabin, I have had time to think and to understand a great many things that were hidden from me before, How can I know my neighbors if I do not know myself? How can I understand my country — and through it the world — if I do not understand those who comprise it? A nation, as I have said before, is only a collection of individuals and the world only a collection of nations. It is very simple, but we wise men disdain that which is not complicated — just as we disdain those things for which we do not have to pay. The sun, the flowers, the birds, the trees are all about us with a wealth of knowledge to give us, but we would rather sit indoors and see a "movie" which can add nothing to our lives except, perhaps, stale sentiment. We have not the remotest idea about how to live, and then we are hurt and surprised when our time comes and we can look back only on "a vale of tears." I have learned something of living here and because I have been given that opportunity, I feel that I am among the most fortunate ones on earth.

The time of life is short;
To spend that shortness basely were too long.

Just looking around me now as I sit in this wood on a great cedar stump hundreds of years old, I feel that the beauty and the riches of this world are almost more than I, in my littleness, can bear. There is so much to see, so much to do, so much to learn and understand. Many times I have stood among the pre-Cambrian rocks and thought of those hundreds of millions of years when there was no life on this earth at all. Now there is life and even I have been granted it. A great gift: so precious that I am the biggest of all fools if I waste even a moment.

The cedar stump where I am sitting is close by the second level above the river and I notice several pieces of granodiorite, chert and greenstone. A former lumber camp is some distance below —

at the edge of the Teal — with white and purple asters, golden-rod, great mullein, ox-eye daisy and golden ragwort growing around it. Clotbur and hedge mustard make the small-flowered lady's thumb, on which Our Lady is supposed to have left her imprint, seem more delicate by comparison with their coarse-ness. Nearby are blue elderberry bushes. This fruit was used by the Indians, as I use it now, for pies, jellies and syrup; but they also made a tea and medicinal concoction from the blossoms and flutes, whistles and bows from the wood. Lewis and Clark probably referred to it when they mentioned an "alder" with "pale sky blue berries," for they were at that time in a part of the country which contains what we call elderberries today. Here it is a fairly low shrub in some places and in others a young tree, although I have never seen one with its trunk even a foot in diameter in this district. It is the silvery bloom on the dark berries which gives them their "pale sky blue" appearance.

Except for the one grove of almost pure evergreens, there have been deciduous trees with me nearly all the way and now there are still more. It is warm and still and green in this place, and the old wagon road is soft under my feet with moss and creeping plants. My feet make no sound on the velvet carpet and when a migrant red-winged blackbird flies across my path, he does not break the silence. This is the second surprise of the day, for these gay gentlemen usually travel in flocks and not often through my territory. But even though he is in the more somber hues of autumn, the day is brighter for his passing.

Then suddenly I am at the end. The trail is blocked by great boulders for several hundred yards and on the other side it is overgrown and tangled with many rockslides. But this is the proper ending anyway. Almost on the path a proud Douglas fir goes up for over one hundred feet against the blue sky, with the sun directly behind it and the mountains green and then blue in the distance beyond. Little puffy white clouds contrast with the intense blue, and whorls of white aphids spiral in the still September air. Blue elderberries hang in clusters and the yellow bur marigold illumines the green foliage of bush and leafy tree. A squirrel is playing happily in a vine maple, like a child before it is gripped by life in the world. A vesper sparrow wings silently across the path and as I turn my head to watch him, I see beyond the fir to where Snow mountain, highest of the Endahwins, gleams white against the sky. Then I know that it will not be long before the snow bunting and the mountain chickadee take the place of the hermit thrush and black-headed grosbeak I saw around my cabin this morning. The rosy finch and I will watch the ducks as they fly down the Wren and the Teal for the last time and one night I shall awaken in the chilly dark to hear the far, fierce cadence of the wild geese going over.

8

End
and beginning

Go, and catch a falling star,
Get with child a mandrake root.

JOHN DONNE

Now the sky is that deep, heart-stirring blue that comes only at this season. It is faintly echoed in the smoke and haze of the October air and in the gray-blue scarves of mist that sometimes encircle the shoulders of the hills. Summer has not yet gone, winter has not yet come. The wind of autumn is filled with welcome and regret.

The days have moved so calmly and warmly from September that it is startling to look up at the mountains and see sun where no sun is and a leap of flame beside it. Frosted-blue elderberries patch the clearings and in the garden three seasons mingle. Beside the diminished pinks, pale blues and mauves stand the dominant reds and yellows, while the white of aster and zinnia is like a drift of snow across the beds. This is the last flare of light before the sun goes down behind the mountains until February and no matter how dark the day, to go out is like entering into sunshine. Lamplight yellow and fire scarlet are everywhere in the valley and each hill is lighted by the flame and golden candles of willow, cottonwood and maple. The sun is in the valley only five hours at most and the grass is never completely dry after the heavy dews of night. It adds a crystal note to the golden days and catches the last light of evening as it falls across my garden.

Time has a slumberous quality, and it is difficult to do more than lie half-asleep in the sunlight, which will soon be gone, or sit idly beside the rivers watching willow gold splatter upon the swift, shallow water. The tensions of dry and busy summer relax. It is pleasant to follow the flight of a leaf spiraling lazily from tree to ground or watch the rain drifting softly over Evergreen and Fireweed mountains. The eyes are mesmerized into sleep by the effortless flow of water, and its sound is more soothing than any lullaby. Sometimes it is low and gentle like a song before dreaming; again, the clear notes of a violin seem to rise into the night air or a symphonic storm comes through the darkness. It is possible to hear every instrument, with now and then quartets and choruses adding their melody to the whole.

I love music deeply, yet I can say that no music I have ever heard can equal these river harmonies. There is nothing so pure, so melodious, so altogether free. But sometimes, in the deep night, a young boy's clear whistle goes down a mapled street and for one black moment I am sick with longing for twenty years of youth and health gone by. Not even to live my life over, but just to live it again. And again.

In the early morning Fireweed resembles that rose city of the desert, Petra. There are few evergreens on the fire-scarred slopes, but small deciduous trees cover the ground like a pastel rug flung down for the light feet of dawn. When the sunrise reflects on them the effect is magical; even the stones are bright rose while the brown earth has changed to glowing amethyst. The clouds are colored delicately pink and golden by a sun that has already risen in lower places, but here all is mist and shadow. The mountain has a silver diaphanous curtain stretched entirely across it from behind, which the lovely red of swamp maple and the yellow of poplar and willow show through in delicate light shades. The colors shimmer as the curtain moves gently, swayed by the slight morning breeze, while on every side of me as I stand on the knoll they are repeated in stronger, bolder tones as they come to me clearly with no mist between. The river murmurs amicably to itself and there is a feeling of contentment everywhere. A varied thrush is a bronze bell ringing in the forest as the wrens tie silver ribbons of song around this autumn painting that the river has wrapped so softly.

Then the sun has risen almost to the top of Cougar and the mists that drift slowly across Evergreen are illumined by it. One dark cloud is in the sky to contrast with the white wraiths below that shift and change, spread and contract, swaying in their graceful dance to the sun. Through them the dark-green sides of the mountain show, with here and there a flash of yellow marking the course of willow and cottonwood along the banks of the dry streams, which will soon be pouring their swifter and colder mist down from the summit. Then the sun rises higher and emerges over the crest of Cougar mountain. The wraiths become quite transparent, the dark cloud is replaced by white, fleecy ones and Evergreen stands out in its habitual emerald beauty. A flock of rosy finches comes down on the stumps, and a late hermit thrush gives a cracked, muted whistle. The juncos — those "black snowbirds" — are here again, this time in company with flocks of nuthatches, warblers and vireos. Mountain chickadees whisper together in the roots of a fallen fir.

These are the days when Birds come back . . .
To take a backward look.

Butterfly, bee and even the great blue damselfly are everywhere in almost as great numbers and variety as in summer. Blue, white, marble, anglewing, swallowtail, tortoiseshell, mourning cloak and the gorgeous red admiral skim across marigold and cornflower, while a flock of golden-crowned kinglets comes sibilantly to the top of a tall cedar.

During the day Fireweed is a brilliant tapestry woven in intricate gradations of autumn somberness and light. It hangs in front of me as I work and I cannot believe that, east or west, there is another mountain more beautiful. Then at twilight, when the mists return, Fireweed becomes an oil painting done by a great master. The veil between gives a touch of enchantment, softening every outline and blending every color into perfection. Beauty veiled is even lovelier than beauty displayed. The air does not have the silken touch of summer; it is more like chiffon and with the same clinging quality. It wraps itself around me and is filmy-delicate against my cheek and hand.

Walking along leaf-strewn paths (my heart always quickens at the sight and scent of my own path redolent of leaves, perhaps because of the many autumn paths I have known that were not mine and never could be), I can feel, already, the first stirrings of separation between my small domain and the world beyond it. Perhaps it is the silence of the woods or the growing river cadences that surround me. Perhaps it is the early darkness or the sharp knife of wind from the uplands cutting the last ties of gay and singing summer. However it is, it is a welcome feeling. Time now for thoughts and dreams, for river concerts and the grand salon of autumn. Time, too, to visit strange countries, stranger than those which are the meccas of the tourists.

Perhaps the strangest of all is the Land of Mist. Its territory extends across my mountains, and I watch it turn first one and then the other into muted autumn landscapes framed in blue. Then, swiftly, a white curtain falls across the picture and when it lifts again only a small section of pale green shows through. It is an astonishing thing to see the sudden lightening of a dark coniferous mountain, piece by piece, as the mist touches it. At first I thought that surely these must be alders that had not yet lost their leaves, but no they were firs and hemlocks and cedars—all with the brightness of spring on them for a few fleeting moments.

When I sit gazing out at Evergreen on these opal mornings, every moment is changed as the misty vapor moves up this valley and through that defile, stealing among the trees and etching a sharp green spire upon an ivory background. Sometimes the treetops are like tiny islands in a restless gray sea; at others, ghosts stand pale and silent in a plasmic ether. The mountain is one mountain no longer, but a whole range with canyon, butte and precipice changing and interchanging. Then, as I look, the sun comes lance-like through, striking the mist to dazzling porphyry and white-shafted gray in spears of light thrown across the immobile slope. But only for a breath. The vapor moves uneasily to and fro and then, dramatically, the whole great curtain is flung upward on a huge puff of wind.

Now the mist has no rest at all. The wind hurries it up this canyon and down that, tosses it over the sunlit peaks, drops it swiftly into a valley and then, recanting, pushes it violently up a stream bed toward the summit once again. After which, with equal abruptness, the wind goes off on other business, the curtain flashes down and Evergreen Theater is closed to me until the next performance. The rivers for my symphony, the mountains for my stage, masterpieces crowded upon my walls — what is there in the greatest cities that I could ever miss?

But Evergreen has become a stranger to me — a beautiful, mysterious stranger in filmy garments — and if I should walk the old familiar trails, perhaps I would be lost among alien formations and ultramontane landmarks. Yet what a temptation! To go behind that curtain, to walk in hidden security back of that nubiferous wall and see the world below in softened loveliness! No harshness there, no sharp corners; only muted sounds and mellow, argillaceous scenes.

And so, of course, I go. By the light of a cloudy autumn day I climb the lower slopes and, for a little while, everything is as it has always been. Then one more step upward and I am in an alien land. Shadowy forms close in around me, the air is dense with moisture, and the sharp scent of it is completely different from the drier, woodsy smell below. Nothing is the same. Old landmarks are gone and the new ones shift constantly. Here is a deep canyon, filled to the brim with fog, where I never knew one to be before. There is a promontory of trees and rocks appearing to overhang a milky gulf below. Then vapor, like an eraser, moves across the whole and for a clear instant afterward the way is as I knew it. I take a deep breath and prepare to go on confidently, but before I can put one foot in front of another I see coulee, headland and mesas appearing and disappearing all around me and there is no certainty anywhere.

I am a prisoner within feather walls with only ghosts for company. I can walk through the walls, but I can never reach the other side. They give before me like the enveloping tactics of war and politics — and also with destruction as the ultimate end for the surrounded if the way is lost. It would be easy to succumb to panic and run frantically from the faceless things behind; to beat impotent hands against nebulous barricades and cry out hollowly. Claustrophobia is here, companioned by the twin fears of darkness and the unknown.

But the solidity that my surroundings lack seems to have gone into the air I breathe. My nostrils and lungs are clogged with it. Hands and face are wet and my clothes beaded with moisture.

The trail underfoot is slippery with mud and the stones damply dark. Moss and creeping plants are a vivid green, with saturated earth showing deep brown between them. But even these things are not tangibles.

I raise my foot expecting to bring it down on solid ground and find myself sliding on the gravel of a small incline where the mist is lying in wait to trip me. I expect a rise and come sharply flat with the jar and foolish feeling experienced on that disappearing step of a dark stairway. Trees and bushes pop up like genii three inches from my face, but when I reach out to touch one beside the trail it fades as quietly and completely as the Cheshire cat or my acquaintance, the cougar. I would not identify on oath any part of this opalescent land. There is nothing here that I have known or will ever know again.

Every sound is muffled and sight is a strange, uncertain thing. Then wonderfully, I am at the summit, on a huge rock in a place devoid of trees. The sun flashes through, leaving me in a clear world above a shifting vaporous sea. I am out in space with the globe of earth so far below me that even the battle cries cannot reach me now, and at last I know why each religion has placed its heaven in the sky. I am cut off from all familiarity and here is a warm, bright land of space where time has blended into eternity. It will not be an easy thing to plunge down into that gray country once more and through it to the tired, habitual earth.

October means that ax and saw will be heard constantly in the forest, and the woodshed will bulge with maple, alder, cedar, fir and hemlock. Log piles rear up in nearby clearings and by windfalls everywhere. Withered perennials are cut down and bulbs planted in the ground. As always, past and future mingle with the present. Fruit preserving is over, but there are dills and sauerkraut to be put up and vegetables to be canned and pickled. The big crocks and the sealers of red, white and green spiciness join high-piled boxes of root vegetables in the crowded storage house. Beans, peas and every sort of seed are drying in cotton bags above the stove. Herbs hang from the porch roof or lie on trays in the oven, according to the weather. Squirrel-like, stores are piled up against the winter so that the goodness of the earth may still be present even when the snow lies deep and steady on the ground.

SILENCE IS MY HOMELAND

There's rosemary and rue; these keep
Seeming and savour all the winter long.

The days quicken as they move on into late October. Fires are kept lighted outside and in, and their smoke films the clear, crisp air. The great bush piles crackle and spit by day and at night become giant smudges, now and then thrusting out a swift orange tongue at the darkness. Squirrels and chipmunks run vertically through the woods; water ouzels ballet dance on the stones of the river or skim the cooling stream like swift gray arrows. But in the forest time still moves slowly. Moss and fern and creeping vine are green, with the red berries of twisted-stalk and starflower burning against them. No leaf rustles underfoot where only evergreens stir overhead. The wildflowers of summer have gone, but aster, goldenrod, thistle, hawkweed, moonshine and sunflower still star the slopes and clearings. Cottonwood and aspen have turned now and bring sunshine to replace the sun. Both days and nights are chill and the rivers are coming into fuller voice. As the sun dips low behind the mountains, the moon rides high. Sometimes it is barred with clouds and then Fireweed will be ebon save for a great silver gash across its flank, or Evergreen will be in shadow except for an argent spray laid on its crest. These nights are among the loveliest on earth.

There is still no feeling of darkness or approaching winter, for the nights close to the full moon are light enough to walk anywhere without a lantern, even when the sky is covered with clouds. But it will not be long now before the sun is down behind Evergreen, the leaves are fallen from the trees and there are no colors in all the world but brown, dark green, ivory of mist and black of rain cloud. In the dark of the moon night will be a great cave where gloom recedes only a little before the light in my hand.

The voice of the rivers is the one constant sound that breaks the stillness after the birdsongs are hushed and the winds have not yet come. In spite of the swiftness that underlies it, the voice of the Teal has a constant, serious, almost stately measure. It takes with some solemnity the journey to the larger Mallard, but the day I might have drowned in it I felt the full force of its ironic humor. It knocked me off my feet and then, after a few moments of current under chill dark water, sent me spinning into the bank at the other side. Just a little lesson to warn me against future carelessness. Two days later a man fell from a footlog a mile above and his body was found three miles below my cabin. There was no humor in the Teal then. The little Wren is a different case. Its voice has no continuity, but chortles and gurgles and goes up and down the scale. It always seems to be having a great deal of fun, with no particular plan in life — and even if it had one I doubt if it would care very much. Even in spring and fall, when it is large and yellow and a bit grim, I always feel that it might still be induced to play a while with me. But I would hesitate to suggest such a thing to the dignified Teal. Yet, with their bass and treble that harmonize so well, my two rivers are excellent companions — musically and otherwise.

It is at this time that the last fruits are picked: the bright rose hips that hang from their somber bushes like fairy lanterns. I walk even as far as the village for them, bringing back big dunnage bagfuls to make into sweet, dark-red syrup to replace the vitamin C of the orange and tomato juice I cannot buy. The flavor is so delicious — with very little sugar necessary — that I could drink a tumbler of the syrup with pleasure. Its appearance is that of burgundy. Owing to the recession of the sun from the valley in late summer, I am unable to ripen many tomatoes although a great many green ones go into relishes for winter spreads.

Once I picked rose hips by moonlight and that was a magic thing. The bag was as light as thistledown on my shoulders when I came singing home along Village Road in the crisp October night. A man I met on the way cried out to me in great amazement: "What! Working as late as this!" and I was astonished to think that what I had been doing could be called by such a name. But even if it could, I have never been able to understand why work should always be considered a curse and a burden. It can be both, of course, but then so can everything else in this world which is just beginning to learn its ABCs.

The man who shirks on the job, who fails to finish what he starts, who feels that anything is good enough thinks that he is stinting on toil to have more pleasure, whereas he is really turning his back on one of life's greatest satisfactions. Children have no idea that there is any difference between work and play until that conception is given to them by their parents and other adults. I have watched girls and boys labor in a vegetable patch for hours, unpack and carry fragile china and glass — without a casualty, because they were trusted — up a flight of stairs for half a day and pore over botanical specimens and their explanations with such intensity that even a call to lunch meant nothing — all that without any idea that the whole thing was not the best sort of fun. If a foolish adult had said: "My, what hard work you are doing!," they would probably have sagged at both ends and thrown the whole thing over.

Another error made by so many is in thinking that the particular sort of work they do is the best in the world and should have the most honor. The man who works with his hands looks down on the man who does only mental labor — and the other way around. The artist who paints day and night for three days and then takes the rest of the week off is considered to be shiftless and slightly insane. The individual who actually sits and thinks has a hard time keeping his more officious neighbors from railroading him into the asylum, in their minds at least. Yet it is all good, honest labor — if it is honestly done — and all necessary. For it is not the type of work or even the result of it that is important; it is the doing of it well. Perhaps someone else will pick it up where we have had to drop it; perhaps it can never be finished. That does not matter. For the time being it is ours and we can pour into it all our hopes and dreams and knowledge and skill. It is good even when we are working simply for ourselves or our families, but when we feel that we are working for humanity, that is the ultimate reward. It does not matter, either, whether our particular piece of work is big or small. If it adds one little drop to knowledge, if it raises the level of mankind by the slightest degree, if it causes one person to say: "That comforts me," then nothing can surpass it in importance.

We are inclined to take work too much for granted, to look on it either as a nuisance or an enemy. It is the best friend we ever had. If everyone were suddenly forbidden to do any labor at all, even while still being provided for, most of us would shatter the heavens with our outcries against such hardship and injustice. Then if a few at a time were allowed to go back to work again, we would consider that they were the privileged of the earth. And that is exactly what they would be.

But all these October nights, whether illuminated softly by the stars or floodlighted by the moon, are not spent in what the world calls work. This is the time when a warm feeling of coziness begins to take possession of the little cabin. All spring and summer it has been like another room of the outdoors, but now it is something separate and dear in its own right. My bunk — which is just the width of a pullman berth and always reminds me of one, giving me that same feeling of comfort and privacy — lies in a pool of lamplight with the white sheets and pillowed backrest inviting me to spend another hour or so in creative work or in browsing through this book or that. Or perhaps I feel that it is the perfect time in which to write good friends, telling them something of my other companions here who stand straight and tall in the forest or who speak wisely to me from between publishers' covers.

For out of olde feldes, as man seith,
Cometh all this new corn from yeer to yeer,
And out of olde books, in good feith,
Cometh all this newe science that men lere.

I wonder then how many of us ever sat down to think out exactly what it means to be a friend. It is one of the biggest responsibilities in the world, yet it is undertaken so lightly and abandoned on such slight pretext that it might be the putting on or taking off of a garment. There is, to me, one true reason for friendship and one only: that here is another soul to whom I can give and from whom I can receive the utmost in spiritual value. There can be clarity, stimulation and the ultimate in truth between us. I know what my friend is and he knows what I am. Nothing can alter that — not anything that has happened before or anything that may come afterward.

The past is no concern of either, except as it can strengthen the fabric of our relationship. What comes in the future should no more be able to disturb our amity than a twig dropped on the surface of a great river can alter its course and destiny. Yet what do we see all around us? Friendships — or so they are called —

made because of money, prestige, loneliness, popularity, community of trivial interests, propinquity, business association and for other equally unreliable reasons. There is also that most dangerous of all: the friendship made because each member to it has endowed the other with qualities that are not there. This is dangerous because it usually involves feelings which are both deep and sincere and so it can cause much emotional turmoil and unhappiness. It can also embitter both of them and shadow their lives with distrust because each fails to realize that it is not his friend who has failed him, but he who has failed his friend.

These dream friendships are much more prevalent than is generally believed. They usually rest on the hypothesis that the other person sees life as we see it and so cannot possibly commit a major act of which we will disapprove. Of course, when the "friendship" is trivial, even a minor act will upset it. The result is that when we discover that our friend has committed such an act in the past or at the time we knew him, then he can no longer be our friend. But in what way has he changed that we should look at him with cold eyes and close the door of our heart against him? He is the same as he always was. Those qualities for which we loved him are still there — if they were there at all.

If we thought it through we would know that what he has done he did not consider to be wrong or he could not have done it. He simply has a different way of looking at life — and who can say that just because ours may be the more conventional one that it is, in all cases, correct? But the sorrow should be ours because we led him to believe that we were his friend when, in reality, we were nothing of the sort.

If any man has done wrong the harm is his own, but perhaps he has not done wrong.

Or perhaps our friend does feel that he has erred. Are we to abandon him, then, just when he needs us most? Fine friends we are! How can we hope that there will be anyone to stand by us in *our* weak moments? This would be a good time to sit down and ask ourselves some questions: are we so insecure in ourselves that we are afraid that association with someone who has done wrong may upset our own scaffolding? Or could it be that we know that the neighbors will disapprove of our friend and we have not the courage to be seen with him when they will not?

Before friendship I ask myself: can I be a friend? That is the crux of the matter. Then I ask myself: can I be a friend to this certain person? If the answer is "yes," then I let nothing stand in the way of that friendship. I try to see clearly, act honestly, speak sincerely. I try to show myself as I am and to see my friend as he is. The ways of friendship differ with the individuals, but two things should never change: that there is only one reason for making a friend and no reason at all for abandoning one.

It is when

I see the cloud-born squadrons of the gale,
Their lines of rain like glittering spears deprest . . .

that the companionship of books becomes a specially cherished thing, for then everything draws within itself a little and, except for the flooding rivers, there is silence. Work moves indoors, and the furniture and windowsills receive an additional coat of paint against the smoke of winter fires. The cabin seems to become more compact and secluded. No visitors will arrive through the rain-drenched woods, and a feeling of security and calm falls manna-like upon the heart. In the companionship of great minds the world's voice is only a shouting far behind.

Now it is possible to look upon one's own face with leisured scrutiny. Outside, the sunless days are like a Chinese print. Cottonwoods etched on smoke or against the silver mists of the mountain seem like something out of faery. Everything is line, now that color has gone, and the good bones show the expert modeling of the earth. The spirit of man is quiet and apart, for there is substance to be drawn from these shadowy days when the rain, steadily and softly, lulls unreason and unrest to sleep.

Now there is more shadow than light anywhere and in the night the wild geese, crying on the scent of summer lost, go swiftly over. The next morning the ground is white and the bushes are encased in silver. It is the first heavy frost of the year. The air has a sparkle to it and the rivers, running by their white-rimmed stones, seem to have been chilled in ice. The sun arrives for its hour in the valley, and the ground begins to steam around the stiff brown plants in their nests of mulch. Bushes are transformed into crystal figurines and the tips of the sword fern glint sharply. The steam is like incense rising from the earth until the sun goes and there is chill and shadow once again. At night the frostlight is on the darkened river, flowing like ebony between silver banks under the polished steel of all the stars of heaven. The stars are so brilliant that they light the cabin with their silver glow. The old moon, with "the young moon in her arms," swings from a clear dark sky, and frost glitters delicately under the ray of my flashlight.

At half past seven on a later morning stars and moon are there again; except to the east where the sky has paled before the first thrust of dawn. Light sparkles on the grass and bushes, becoming a white dust everywhere as the daylight deepens. Finally sunlight touches the highest point of Evergreen mountain and sends a great shaft pointing from the last edge of the gap between that mountain and Cougar. But in ten weeks more it will cross the gap in full view and begin to climb the sky. Even now the sunrises and sunsets hold great loveliness as the saffron clouds drift like smoke across the mountaintops, changing to pale yellow and finally to ivory before they disappear. Standing on the knoll just as Mars opens his red eye beside Cougar and a white hoarfrost cloud drifts down the Teal, I can sense that serene music of autumn which accompanies the singing of the rivers and gray wings turning the year's torn page.

This is the month when the stars go on their long shift and the moon becomes more enticing than ever because of the bare darkness of the world around. Coming down Main Street from the train at about three one moonlit morning, I found the forest an enchanted place. Gold and scarlet leaves still clung precariously to vine and broadleaf maple in

That time of year . . .
When yellow leaves, or none, or few, do hang
Upon those boughs which shake against the cold.

and the green of the forest floor was much more carpet than underbrush. The moon was so bright that it did not silver the objects around, but made the leaves glow like shaded lamps of rose and pale yellow above a dark-green rug. Moving toward an open glade from the shadows was like moving toward the Holy Grail, and I could understand then how it might have seemed to

the old prophets that God appeared to them in such heavenly
light as that shafted from the sun or from such a moon as this.
Looking at this illuminated glade, mystical and silent in the
center of darkness, I felt the silver finger of November's beauty
laid gently on my heart.

November has a strong, clean smell. Damp leaves and water
are in it, with wet earth and bracken adding a light, evasive
perfume to the nights and days. But the chief constituent is
wood. It is possible now to distinguish, especially in the evenings
and early morning, between the pungency of cedar and the tang
of fir, the bitterness of hemlock and the mildness of willow. It is
something which is present at no other time of year with such
clarity. It opens up a whole new olfactory world, and my nostrils
twitch in all directions trying to record and catalogue each odor.
Wood and water — what perfect ingredients for a perfume! Here
is relaxation of the earth: that quiet resting after the labor and
turmoil of summer and the spaded disturbance of early fall. I
draw long, deep breaths of fulfillment and content. The river
scent is in my nostrils and my eyes are soothed by the cool,
soft-stepping November wind.

But sometimes, after the sun has definitely retreated to his
mountain heights and my valley is wet once more with the dews,
rains and melting frosts that will not dry again until spring, my
mind becomes restless and my feet begin to itch for outland trails.
I look up at the snowy summit of Fireweed and know that there is
a strange, exciting land that must be visited — a sparkling country of sunshine surrounded by bright blue sky and with a little
mountain wind which blows glistening dust through white de-
files and along immobile streams.

Shadows and moisture go with me as I walk up Main Street
and along Village Road. Everything I touch is saturated and
globules hang from each leaf and stem. I walk west on Village
Road for half a mile and then turn sharply up the slope of
Fireweed where a mountain stream bed makes climbing possible
at this steep part that I have chosen. No gentle rise here as at
Bill's, where the slope finally declines almost to a hill, but a great
flare of rock and underbrush rising more than two thousand feet
above me.

For the first thousand feet it is like any rough mountain scramble. It is not time to turn and look down on the way behind, for I have not yet crossed the frontier into my strange land. Then suddenly I am there. The steep path levels out a little and I stand on white snow in dazzling sunlight to look back on the shadowed territory I have left behind. An old river bed of the Teal crosses my stream at this place and from here to the summit a network of creek and gravel benches makes a more gradual ascent possible, although such a course will mean going a mile or so westward compared to the quick, sharp climb to the peak just above me. But the longer way is the way for me! What is the use of entering a foreign country at all — unless, of course, just to say that one has been there — if you do not explore it properly? And what a country it is! Ruby of vine maple, topaz of willow, dark emerald of conifer, garnet of western dogwood, pearl of snowberry — a jeweled land displayed upon white velvet. These treasures line my path and, if I dared, I would touch each one and gloat over it and become quite delirious with joy.

This snowfall was the first of the year and only a few inches deep. At first it is wet and clinging, but as I go higher it becomes powdery and dry while the air lightens and quickens. The mountain wind, which is hardly ever absent from these high places, sends silver eddies spiraling and touches my cheek with sharp-pointed fingers. But the sun is like a great fire burning on these high, white hearths and I am soon stripped to light undershirt and ski trousers — with serious thoughts of getting down to the shorts underneath the latter. The sky is burning also, with a clear blue flame untempered by any cloud, and the air is sauterne in a crystal goblet. I am glad of my sunglasses, for the brilliance of sun on snow is blinding to a valley dweller in winter shade. Sometimes a powder flurry drifts across my face or marks with a faint sweeping the virgin way ahead. I never fail to thrill at the sight of my own footsteps signing a blank expanse, although I would prefer to see the long sweep of ski tracks ribboning behind me. That is, to me, the great way to travel in winter, but it is not possible in many parts of this country where too often clog snow and stumps are everywhere.

Twice I have been lost in the mountains: once in snow and once in fog. That is an experience that leaves a cross of memory on the brain which no time or will can ever quite wear away. Yet perhaps a writer is better equipped for such a trial than many others, for the refusal to give up hope is the best weapon one can have — and what writer with years of rejection slips behind him could ever succumb easily to despair? Even now I can hardly bring myself to speak too seriously of those hours when I plodded through fog and snow — once with moisture heavy and stifling on my breath, once with snow a fist in my eyes and a vampire at my lungs — not knowing whether all this weariness was for nothing and I would find myself back at the beginning again or at the end. There was panic to fight and the hurry which induces it; there was that dreadful temptation to lie down and let sleep flow over or to sit with the mind blank and no wish ever to get up again.

Once there was darkness and hunger, with wrenching cold to steal the breath and paralyze the limbs, yet they were realities to be dealt with and so almost a relief. But despair is the great enemy, for it numbs the mind with its false logic of futility and so, in time, the body also. Whatever those who are drowning may do, let them never think of the past when they are lost. Let them think of the present keenly and of the future surely, but let old days be a deep well with a cover on it unless they contain a lesson that can be put to use at once. No, I cannot speak of those times even now and even though I was strong in them — strong until I saw a familiar landmark and went down on the ground because suddenly my legs would not hold me any more or my mind will me to stand upright. My heart, which had hammered and raced and been quieted almost forcibly, seemed to swell for a moment and skip a beat. Then it went on normally again, if a little wearily, and so did I.

But in the sun and snow of Fireweed on this late November day there is no chance of fog or snowstorm or a lost trail. It is all light and warmth and happiness. Color is still strong on trees and bushes right to the very crest and when I reach there, hot and breathing deeply from my last quick spurt, I know what the kingdoms of the world must have looked like to Jesus. From east to west the dark thread of the Teal stitches a green cloth and seems almost to pass through lovely Snow mountain of the Endahwins. Across from me, to the south, Evergreen raises its somber strata with a dusting of snow on the peak which is a few hundred feet lower than mine. I can see the valley where the village lies, while to the north waves of mountains roll away from me like a great white sea.

> *How often we forget all time, when lone,*
> *Admiring Nature's universal throne,*
> *Her woods, her wilds, her waters, the intense*
> *Reply of hers to our intelligence.*

Sometimes, when I have been sleeping on a mountaintop, I have felt that I must reach up and draw the moon down into my arms. Now I would like to wrap the blue sky around me, warm my hands at this high sun and then reach out to touch each peak; to pat it gently on the head and say: "I am here and I love you." Even the strongest — perhaps especially the strongest — need to have that said to them at times.

> *He who ascends to mountain-tops, shall find*
> *The loftiest peaks most wrapt in clouds and snow;*
> *He who surpasses or subdues mankind*
> *Must look down on the hate of those below.*

Perhaps loneliness of the spirit is the hardest cross to bear, but there is serenity in it as there is in the loneliness of the mountains. That is when we have found ourselves. Most of us go through our whole lives without ever knowing who we are. Our opinion of ourselves is, too often, formed by the opinions others have of us, or our dreams have made it our wishful thinking. I have said this before in different ways, but it is something that seems so tremendously important that I cannot help saying it again in this way. Our parents and teachers tell us that we are thus and that we must try to be so. We take their word for it and try very hard. Perhaps they are right in what they say, but perhaps they are wrong, for the world of today is not the world of tomorrow and what may be regarded as unshakable as the mountains on Monday may by Tuesday have become only a drift of rockdust passing almost unnoticed across the landscape. That is a discovery which is made by many of us as we grow older — it would save us much unhappiness if we could make it sooner — but we seem unable to pass it on to those who come after us. Perhaps it is because, like Dunsany's travelers on the road of the priests, we think that the temple of knowledge we enter is the only one for future generations to inhabit. Very few of us resemble that one traveler who passed by all the temples until he came to the deep chasm and the little god who cried: "I know not!"

When we can say that we do not know, it is the beginning of our self-knowledge. But we are so positive. We run a little way up one road, sure that it is the only one for us, only to find that it ends in an impenetrable thicket or a rockslide. Without a thought as to the why of that happening, we turn and run up another road — and another — and another. We are not paying so much attention to the guideposts of our parents and teachers now, but our neighbors are always more than willing to tell us the way we should take.

We become quite desperate in our efforts to follow their instructions, so that we shall not be left behind or find ourselves on a strange path alone. How dreadful that would be! So the years go by, spent in believing that others know what we are and what we should do. But most of them are abysmally ignorant of themselves and their own destinations, so how can they direct us intelligently? Perhaps by chance or, for the few, by intent the roads they follow are the right roads for them, but that does not mean that they are right for us. When it is too late we may look back and find that those strange, lonely paths were the ones we should have followed after all.

But if it is not too late, if we can stop our aimless running and sit down to look ourselves squarely in the face, what do we want to put into life; what do we wish to get out of it? Shall it be one god or many or none at all? Why, there is a life to be lived and time is not long enough for it! So having found out what sort of people we are, we can take our first steps on the road that is right for us. Perhaps it is well traveled; that will make the going a great deal easier. But perhaps it is a briery, stony path with only the faintest marks to show that anyone has gone that way before. The lonely trail seems even lonelier because the neighbors, furious because we have flouted their advice and terrified of anyone who is "different," have decided that stones and spit will bring us back to the highway. In their anger and fear they may have us imprisoned; they may even kill us.

But to those who know themselves and their way, disgrace and even death do not matter. Jesus was not the first nor the last to be reviled and crucified. He was not the first nor the last to be scorned by his own generation and honored by those that followed. If that is consolation, then we have it. But the greatest consolation will come from seeing clearly the path for us and following it. That will give us strength, courage and understanding to enrich ourselves and others, for the better we know ourselves the better others will wish to know us. In spite of tribulation we shall, perhaps, be as close to happiness as it is possible to come. Whether it is the traveled highway or the dim trail does not matter so long as we are sure that it is our way. Those who are weak will always run with the multitude; they will be tossed about by every current and perpetually sidetrack themselves as they look for easier and easier paths to follow. But those of us who come to know ourselves can never be weak again. We are sure where we are going and why, and there is deeper satisfaction in that than in anything else in the world.

There is a great satisfaction to me, also, in having visited my strange, white land and in the feeling that now I can look up at it from below and say: "There is a vine maple, just by that rock I see, with snow holding it like a silver candlestick." Or "There is a great drift just where that stream bed curves, with low willows yellowing its edges like those of an old and treasured volume." It was fortunate that I climbed when I did, for a few days later it is the valley that is the mysterious land while the mountains have returned to their habitual ways. Jack Frost, that famous craftsman, comes to my clearing on nightshift, and I wake one morning to find each blade of grass, each leaf and branch silvered beautifully and completely. The leaves of the sweet williams are Jack's special pride, I think, for they turn upward slightly at the edges and so the center groove is in lovely green contrast to the border of soft, pure white. This green is paler than in summer — an ice green really — and the whole gives an effect of delicate exquisiteness that I have never seen equaled by human hands.

Autumn has fallen from the trees to the ground and now the hill tapestry of a little while ago is a carpet underfoot of tempered brown, green, yellow and red. It is frost, not fog, that softens now, lightening everything under its thin glaze until the reds are rose and the yellows almost ivory. In fact, my clearing has be-

come Sugar Plum Land. The flowers in sheltered rockeries and borders resemble nothing so much as those delicious candied fruits of the confectioner's windows. The blue of gentian, the rose of ice plant and the green of both show through the frosted coating and it is all I can do not to nibble them or to pick the toothsome-looking leaves from the small apple trees on the flat and munch them greedily. Frost is most beautiful when it comes before the snow, for then it is in lovely contrast to the dark objects which it decorates. Nevertheless it is all rather confusing.

From a little distance the valley is snow white. The forest is green, the mountains are green. Where last year and the years before at this time Fireweed and Evergreen had candles of crystal lighted on their summits and their rock faces were alabaster and porphyry, this year they are deep emerald with a diamond valley sparkling between them. There is not even a flake left on their peaks of that earlier high snow and where usually in the last days of November the rivers are a turgid flood, this year they are so low that their bones are showing.

Each night my valley is in rehearsal for the Christmas performance. Small evergreens are trimmed with tinsel, icicles and pseudosnow, with lights flashing from the branches whenever my lamp rays touch them. Stars crackle in the sky and hang from the branches of the tallest evergreens. Stars above and stardust below, sprinkled on every bush and tree in the clearing and making even the bark walls of the cabin sparkle. It is like walking among millions of fireflies. The delectable sugar plums are everywhere and when I go out, I feel as though I had stepped straight back into one of my childhood stories where gumdrops grew on trees and the rivers ran with delicious lemonade. Each year I would ask Santa Claus for a present like that, but this is the first year he has given it to me. I must have been very good indeed.

The November darkness that follows the November day is no true darkness, for then the land is quickened and silver-torched by moonlight or by starglow. These nights are like laughter at the wedding feast, for it is nearly that awaited hour when man and winter will be alone together.

9

Wilderness winter

Silence is the perfectest herald of joy:
I were but little happy, if I could say how much.
                                              SHAKESPEARE

Slowly, slowly the evergreen of the mountains has retreated before the steady advance of snow. Then one evening I look out the window and the soft languid flakes are falling in the lamplight. They fall all night, while the voice of the river becomes more and more hushed and the noises of the forest die away. By dawn the whole world of stream and wood and mountain has been kindled to a white flame of beauty.

There is nothing quite like the first snow. I go out in the early morning and there is such silence that even breath is a profanation. The mountain to the north has a steel-blue light on it and to the west the sky still holds something of the darkness of night. To the east and south a faint, very faint, pink is beginning to spread. I look up and see the morning star keeping white watch over a white world.

Soon the whole sky is azure and flamingo, but still the silence holds. Every branch of every tree is weighted with cold and stillness; every stump is crowned with crystal; every fallen log is overlaid with silver. The wild berry bushes have puffballs of jeweler's cotton here and there along their branches and even the stark roots of hemlocks and cedars have become grottos of quartz and chrysolite. And the silence holds.

The sky is clear blue now and the sun has flung diamonds down on meadow and bank and wood. Beauty, the virgin, walks here quietly, quietly. She is telling her pearls, and her feet make no sound and no sign upon the immaculate snow. The silence is dense and deep; it is like nothing else.

Then the night comes, and the silence holds. The moon is high with a dark-blue sky behind it and with mountains, plains and forests of silver lying below. The trees, the bushes and the tall ferns are carved with alabaster; the meadows and lawns are white satin set with diamonds. The earth is whole; it is immutable. In this candid perfection the heart is hushed and even thought seems blasphemy. What mind can hold this beauty? What words can define it? Still the silence holds.

There is a feeling about this season that is in no other. It is a sense of snugness, security and solitude; its "beauty is eternity gazing at itself in a mirror." There will be no human visitors now until spring and nothing to disturb long hours of work and contemplation. Only the bark walls and the windows of the little cabin show between the white-laden roof and the white drifts around, yet the whole building seems to be more solid, more firmly rooted. At night golden lamplights stream out over the snow, and smoke from the fireplace rises straight up into the clear, still air. Such a picture of warmth and contentment! It is hard to know which is better — to be outside looking in at such a scene, or to be inside looking out at the sparkling stars, the bright mountains shouldering a night-blue sky and all the calm clarity of wintered earth.

Sometimes when we are alone we are in the best company. By "alone" I mean away from people, for actually we are never completely by ourselves. Can I say that I am solitary when I may discuss friendship with Emerson, war and peace with Tolstoy, nature with Thoreau and history with Carlyle, Gibbon and a dozen others? Where, in any city or countryside, could I ever hope to find such great minds and gather them around my fireside? Here is company enough to last the winter through and make me forget — if I wished to forget — that my nearest neighbor is separated from me by miles of snow and ice and bitter air. Here are stimulation, strength and warmth for the weakest heart.

A good book is the precious life-blood of a master-spirit,
embalmed and treasured up on purpose to a life beyond life.

Outside, not wishing to disturb us except by their singing now and then are the great trees, the tall mountains, the swift rivers and the winds. What staunch friends and good companions! They are always there and always the same. I can depend on them as I can on nothing else in the world. In winter we see each other clearly and matters are simple and direct between us. In spring we are the helpers in the delivery room and the great experience binds us as nothing else can. In summer we laugh and play and work together and are very merry indeed. I have no time then to miss people or even books and music. Here are the great symphonies of the rivers, night and day. Here is the heart-gripping book of the earth spread out before me, and it is all I can do to read even a part of it before the leaves whisk over and it is autumn. Then we draw very close to each other, my friends and I. We work together to set our house in order, for there is much to be done and much joy in doing it.

"And what is it to work with love? It is to weave the cloth with threads drawn from your heart, even as if your beloved were to wear the cloth. It is to build a house with affection, even as if your beloved were to dwell in that house. It is to sow seeds with tenderness and reap the harvest with joy, even as if your beloved were to eat the fruit. Work is love made visible. And if you cannot work in love, but only in distaste, it is better to leave your work and sit at the gate of the temple and take alms of those who work for joy. For if you bake bread with indifference, you bake a bitter bread that feeds but half a man's hunger, and if you sing though as angels, and love not the singing, you muffle men's ears to the voices of the day and the voices of the night."

These friends of mine have their moods, as I do also — that makes them more interesting — but underneath they never change. With them as with certain books, I have allied myself with those who will never "keep the word of promise to our ear and break it to our hope." Each year it is harder to watch the seasons pass. Each one is so dear that I wish I could keep it with me always. It is like straining for the first glimpse of a beloved face while longing for the first sight of one equally adored.

It is a wrench to find the seas of snow receding and know that winter, which gave me such a sense of warmth and security, will soon be gone. But, later, it is just as difficult to discover that the leaves are losing their first fresh, and paler, green; that the hyacinth smell of bracken is growing fainter; and that the perfume of newly turned damp earth has almost evaporated. Then the first leaves blow past me on the wind and my heart cries for their going, but now the woods are shouting with color and there is the sun to follow. When I have come back from the far trails and look up from putting the flowers to bed, winter is standing beside me. I have had another rich year with my friends.

I would change a quotation and say: "Where there is no *solitude,* the people perish." Each one of us is a well from which we draw the very waters of our life to give to those around us. But one day we find that the well is dry because we have forgotten to go away from the world at intervals and, in contemplation and seclusion, replenish it again. The greatest religions were born near the desert and matured in the wilderness. Man's body is formed in the stillness of the womb and his mind in the privacy of creation.

If "the world is too much with us" we become like parrots, repeating only what we hear and never forming an original sentence for ourselves. Our opinions are so underdone that even the sharpest mental teeth could not get nourishment out of them. Our ideas have as much diversity of color as Jacob's coat and we change them with the dexterity of a chameleon. We are divided into far more parts than Gaul because of the multiplicity of persons and objects around us. We fill every second of our days with things and people, without realizing that we have wasted almost all those hours not spent in sleep.

Soon we are terrified to be alone. We are afraid to look at our own faces in the mirror of contemplation. We talk and talk and say nothing. We can neither give nor receive because we do not know what we want or what gifts we possess. Our lives are like quicksand under our feet because we have never taken the time away from others to explore ourselves and discover where our firm land lies.

This, extended to a people, makes for insanity and gibbering. Not knowing where they wish to go, how shall they recognize the road? Not knowing what they should have, how shall they find it? They cannot look toward the east for dawn because they have lost their sense of direction and no longer know where their sun will rise. They have forgotten the stars in their panic to kick away the stones that might impede their circling progress. They cannot stand firmly anywhere because they do not know where it is they wish to stand. It is indeed true that "where there is no vision, the people perish" — but vision is the favorite child of solitude.

These days of snow in the valley are also days of working inside with plane and hammer and square — building lampstands, another desk and more and more bookshelves. Birdhouses are made and painted, and feeding stations put out at strategic points. Everything that has been broken is mended, and new handles are made for old tools. Patching and stitching go on by lamplight, and the house is put in order for the busy days of spring. The woodshed is kept filled and big blocks are piled up on the side veranda for the fireplace.

Mail is packed in on snowshoes only at long intervals, but a great deal of writing and reading is done. This is the time for it: when the only visitors are the black-capped and mountain chickadee, snowy owl, Alaska robin, wren and snow bunting, and the hours are long and untroubled — but never long enough. Occasional flocks of western evening grosbeaks and redpolls come to call, or more occasionally still I spy a pine grosbeak in my clearing or glimpse the great gray owl flapping through Home Wood at dusk.

At first there is very little snow in the woods, for the early falls have difficulty in penetrating the density of the conifers. But it is on the topmost branches of the trees, making them like ivory candles in dark, carved holders. Ferns, moss and small bushes still show brown and green on the forest floor, yet there is a strangeness here although so little seems to have changed. For one thing, everything is so much more silent. Even the squirrels have stopped their ribald chattering — giving only faint, pathetic cries at intervals — and faint snowbird whisperings seem to emphasize the stillness.

After heavy snowfalls it is the evergreens that are the loveliest, with their great white branches weighted down until they are almost parallel with the trunks. They seem like giant birds with their wings folded against the cold of winter. But after a light fall it is the deciduous trees that are most beautiful. They are so fragile, so ethereal, that it seems even the sound of the rivers might shatter them as they drift like crystal smoke along the banks. The bushes are silver filigree, so light, so much on tiptoe in this enchanted world. Even the slightest breeze sends the snow shimmering down from them, leaving the branches brown and bare and rather pitiful.

Be silent now; perhaps we shall never know
Again this moment of white, arrested peace
Held like a breath on branch and blade and stone
Poised for a thought of muted, cool surcease.
The wind will stir, the bough spring upward sending
Its drifted spray to luster the tempered air;
The foot will cancel the void, the hand go seeking
And what has been will not be anywhere.

All winter long there is the plop-plop of snow shaken by the wind from the laden evergreens. It marks the ground almost like a paw print. But there are other marks as well: rabbit, mouse, cougar, coyote and, occasionally, lynx, weasel and shrew. The scream of a mountain lion or the howling of a coyote is like the voice of the wilderness in the long winter nights. It is impossible to travel in the woods without snowshoes before the hard crust of January forms. You sink down to your knees, to your waist. It is hard to keep the necessary paths cleared, and exercise, except with ax and shovel, is considerably curtailed. But "a snow year, a rich year!"

Anyway, it does not matter. Nothing seems to matter very much in this winter wilderness. The world of people is far and far away and the jittering of it like an unpleasant dream. This is the real world here. There are days like etchings and days like snatches from the ballet of *Swan Lake*. Sometimes, although in December and January there is no sun in the valley, reflections of light from the glittering sides of Fireweed mountain make shadows on the snow and inside the cabin. At night there are shadows also, if not from the sun, then from the stars. They are white, sharp lights in the midnight-blue sky and appear literally to spark with coldness. I feel as though I could see every star in the universe at such times.

The stumps resemble the White Queen more than a little, and the stones in the river are like loaves that have risen beyond all imagination, each one set on a lacy doily of ice. In January parts of the river freeze and the pool, Dubh Glas, is thinly coated. When I break through the ice close to the shore, I find first an opaque substance and then one that is as transparent and delicate as the finest Waterford crystal. In certain lights the forest is not "white with snow," but the pale, elusive blue of the mountain distance. The snow, when I dig into it, has a grotto-blue light below, but when I pick that portion of it up in my hands it is white again. That which cannot be grasped may yet be real.

Winter is such a satisfying time. It is good to go out into the bracing cold, which clears the mind and invigorates the heart. It is equally good to come in and feel the warmth of the house wrap around the body like a soft, fluffy blanket. It is difficult to know which is more enjoyable: coffee on the terrace in June or by the fireplace in December. Fire is a first-rate companion and the black kettle singing on its crane always joins in the conversation. The coffee is full-bodied and fragrant; shadows dance on the walls to make the cedar paneling glow, and the winter world outside my windows is very still. Yes, I am more than content to begin and end a day like this.

So much has been written and sung about the midsummer moon, but to me the midwinter moon is every bit as beautiful — even when the snow is late and only a deep frost lies white upon the ground. Then stepping out into the full moonlight is like entering an exalted springtime for in this brilliancy the grass and unbrowned plant leaves are all pale green below the frost and the conifers emerald through their silver filming. Even the air seems to have taken on a malachite tinge. The moonlight is so powerful that one has a feeling almost of warmth when fully in it. A wild cherry tree stands out like a crystal figurine on a birthday table, in vivid and graceful relief against the dark of Cougar mountain where the moon has not yet come.

Earth and heavens glitter and the sword fern clumps are diamond sunbursts pinned to the silver-sequined ground. But it is all in silence. The chimney smoke rises noiselessly, and the denser drifts from the brushwood fire outside flow upward without a sound. A shooting star flashes across the heavens and that is the strangest silence of all. Even the voices of the rivers are so muffled that one has to listen consciously in order to hear them. This time before the world has become completely white is one of stark magnificence. The undersides of the conifers are still dark green, while the underparts of the many overhanging rocks on Fireweed mountain continue to show deep brown. The whole is a brilliant study in black and white, with silhouette upon silhouette limned against sky and snow.

In winter I do a great deal of burning, giving myself any number of reasons for this preference of season when the real one is that I like to watch a great fire glaring against the snow with the darkness of the forest behind it. There is something elemental and huge about it compared to the small, civilized blaze in my heater. Usually I pile rotten wood, logs and brushwood between stumps that I wish to oust and by the second day the fire has made a cavern for itself underneath the heap, painting the walls,

ceiling and floor a light-red stippled with yellow. Pine branches are the most beautiful of all when burning. The long, bunched needles turn into glowing tassels of golden threads that look as soft as silk. They are soon overlaid with a delicate gray tissue through which the gold pulses like a beating heart.

Fir and hemlock have also their swan song of loveliness as the short, branched needles become rosettes of flame that shimmer and fade along the twigs, transforming each one into a garland for a fire queen's shining hair. At night the flames twist up like glowing wires, which change to dancing sparks as they are blown higher and higher by the fire's hot breath. Sometimes the smoke filters through the forest, bringing out those parts of the trees that it does not cover into eerie, disembodied relief. But sometimes the smoke begins to climb, quickly and steadily, the flanks of Evergreen. Soon it is drifting across the very promontory where I have sat so many times and I feel more than a little envy of such ease and rapidity. In one deep dusk this high smoke caught the last rays of the sun setting in the valley of the village and became the saffron veil of some mysterious houri. One clear, cold night the first rays of an invisible moon transmuted it into a great cobweb of crystal and silver, which surely had been spun by stars and not by fire at all.

The clink of wood split for the small stove is a musical sound, with the notes going higher as one gets nearer the outside of the block, while the wood itself is very colorful against the strong white of winter. The near-rose of cedar, the primrose of rotting hemlock, the clear ivory of fir glow softly upon their perfect background, and I feel that it is almost desecration to take them away from it, giving them in exchange only the prosaic frame of my side veranda. But there are times when that frame is a rare and lovely thing, when beyond my porch a winter sun shows on the far side of Home Wood — a red lamp glinting through needled apertures. Great lengths of citrine and flamingo buntings are thrown up on the sky, and the slight smoke from my chimney drifts gauzily across them — and there is the winter sunset, which so many artists have attempted, held clear and still for one sharp winter moment.

The moonlit nights are vibrant with beauty. Silver comes pouring from the sky to make the bushes molten and snow like diamonds. The river runs like quicksilver between the porcelain of its banks. It seems impossible for one human heart to contain all this loveliness without breaking. Perhaps the ache that is in mine sometimes comes from the knowledge that all this beauty is so ephemeral, that it will be gone before I have done more than touched it with my fingertips.

Not only is it gone so swiftly, but when I try to put it on paper it goes further still. It is so difficult to describe the happiness of simplicity, the joy of little things. Perhaps I sound sentimental and unreal when I write of what the trees, the mountains, the rivers and my little cabin mean to me. I knew when I began that it would be impossible to tell it all or even, perhaps, to put it so that you who read it would feel it running through your blood as I do through mine. If you have felt instead that I was laying wares out for your approval and being emotional about each one as I showed it to you, then my writing has failed indeed.

For there is nothing unreal or sentimental in my heart about these things. They are as simple and natural to me as the bread I eat or the wood I bring to flame. They are in me and I am in them and that is the way it will be always. Even when I was lost in the mountains I was still among friends. I thought that those times might be times of testing, or perhaps it was intended I should die then — and where better could I die than surrounded by those I love?

What is it to cease breathing, but to free the breath from its restless tides; that it may rise and expand and seek God unencumbered?

Perhaps it seems unreal that I should wish to be surrounded by such things rather than by human friends, that I could ever really love them. But I do. There are a few human beings whom I love deeply also — and many, many more whom I like — but even with them the trappings of conventional habit and the nigglings of civilization enter and I cannot feel that utter flowing together, which is the sustenance of the heart. But here in my valley I have felt it ever since the first year. In that first year I had to get rid of a great many useless thoughts and habits, but afterward came the deep certainty, the faith, the utter happiness that seemed to bubble up inside me like the water of life. No, that is not just a simile; it is the truth. It did, it does.

Coming back to this place is like entering a room where friends beyond the best of friends are waiting. Everything is easy and right from the first moment and, no matter how fretted and jarred I may be while away, once I am home the strain slips off as physical weariness disappears in a relaxing bath. Understanding and dependability I have found to be very rare "outside," but here after that first period of adjustment, I have found nothing else. I feel such kinship with everything I touch and see. It is just here — around me all the time like a comforting garment. When the dark moods come, I go into the forest or up on the mountains and then it is almost as if I were drinking courage from some great spring of the subconscious, as though some wise friend, giving me no pity, said: "All this is nothing! The important thing is that there is work for you to do. Why are you wasting time?" Before I know it the happiness, which never really stopped bubbling even at lowest ebb, is springing up again like a fountain with birds singing around it.

Here I have been taught wisdom, I have been made humble. I have known what it is to give myself utterly, in joy and surety, and to receive so unstintingly, so graciously that every moment is thanksgiving — and that not enough. I could never lie down upon the earth and not feel comfort; I could never lean against a tree and not be strengthened; I could never go up in the mountains and not find courage and wisdom. I have gone to people for comfort and received impatience or stupid words; I have leaned and found nothing there; I have searched for wisdom and courage only to find weakness and incomprehension. But not here — never here! I was diseased and lame and blind, but this has made me whole.

Give me my scallop-shell of quiet,
My staff of faith to walk upon,
My scrip of joy, immortal diet,
My bottle of salvation,
My gown of glory, hope's true gage,
And thus I'll take my pilgrimage.

No, it is no use. Here again are words and words, but still the thing I want to say is not said. Some day I may be able to do it: when I am a greater writer and a greater person than I am now. If I become that writer and that person, these friends around me and that Spirit will have made me so.

Sources for Quotations

Sources for the quotations which appear in this book are given sequentially below, arranged by the chapters in which they occur.

Home

Let the fields and the gliding streams — Virgil, Georgics; It is a comfortable feeling — Anthony Trollope, The Last Chronicles of Barset; However small it is on the surface — Charles Dudley Warner, My Summer in a Garden; There is no season — William Browne, "Variety"; Every man hath in his own life — Jeremy Taylor, Holy Living; Never any more to hurry — David Grayson, Adventures in Solitude; . . . after we have made the just reckoning — William Rena, "Some Fruits of Solitude"; The soul selects her own society — Emily Dickinson, "Exclusion"; Henceforth I ask not good fortune — Walt Whitman, Leaves of Grass

SOURCES FOR QUOTATIONS

2   The Blossoming

Now the buds swell — Virgil*; *The levelled lances of the rain* — Paul Hamilton Hayne, "Storm in the Distance"; . . . *Daffodils, | That come before the swallow dares* — Shakespeare, *The Winter's Tale; Whan that Apprille with his shoures sote* — Chaucer, *The Canterbury Tales; For May wol have no slogardye a-night* — Ibid.; *Annihilating all that's made* — Andrew Marvell, "The Garden"

3   Sun in the Valley

Inebriate of air am I — Emily Dickinson, "Exclusion"; . . . *there is no ancient gentlemen but gardeners* — Shakespeare, *Hamlet; Doubtless God could have made a better berry* — Izaak Walton, *The Compleat Angler; In rivers, the water that you touch* — Leonardo da Vinci, from his notebooks, *"Prisoner, tell me* — Rabindranath Tagore, *Gitanjali; Now welcom, somer* — Chaucer, *The Parliament of Fowls; We are all clever enough* — Mimnermus (630-600 B.C.), fragment; *To know that all is well* — Sophocles, *Oedipus Tyrannus; I have no superfluous leisure* — Shakespeare, *Measure for Measure; These, too, are triflers*; I am a true laborer* — Shakespeare, *As You Like It*

4   The Pilgrimage

And smale fowles maken melodye — Chaucer, *The Canterbury Tales;* . . . *forth with pilgrim steps, in amice gray* — Milton, *Paradise Regained;* . . . *a certain jollity of mind* — David Grayson, *Adventures in Solitude;* . . . *want that glib and oily art* — Shakespeare, *King Richard III; God made a little gentian* — Emily Dickinson, "Fringed Gentian"; . . . *his head under his wing* — Anonymous, "The North Wind Doth Blow"; *Stand still, you ever moving spheres of heaven* — Marlowe, *The Tragedy of Dr. Faustus;* . . . *framed in the prodigality of nature* — Shakespeare, *King Lear;* . . . *a cast-iron back, with a hinge in it* — Charles Dudley Warner, *My Summer in a Garden;* . . . *silence more musical than any song* — Christina Rosetti, "Rest"; . . . *deep, blue eyes of springtime* — Heine, "Die Blauen Frühlingsaugen"; *One of the ones that Midas touched* — Emily Dickinson, "The Oriole"; *Songs are sung and tales are told* — Gilean Douglas, "Night Song"; *There is a river in Macedon* — Shakespeare, *King Henry V;* . . . *angling will prove to be so pleasant* — Izaak Walton, *The Compleat Angler*

5   Commissioner of Trails

What canst thou see elsewhere — Thomas a Kempis, *Imitation of Christ;* . . . *the star that bids the shepherd fold* — Milton, "Comus"; *The toad, without which no garden* — Charles Dudley Warner, *My Summer in a Garden; The day shall not be up* — Shakespeare, *King John; I have learned silence from the talkative* — Kahlil Gibran, *Sand and Foam; I have ever loved to repose myself* — Montaigne, "Of Experience"; . . . *there is a good deal of fragmentary conversation* — Charles Dudley Warner, *My Summer in a Garden; Night's candles are burnt out* — Shakespeare, *Romeo and Juliet;* . . . *unutterably bright* — Shelley, "Queen Mab"; . . . *there is a sacred horror* — Victor Hugo, *Ninety-Three; This above all to thine own self be true* — Shakespeare, *Hamlet; Our country, right or wrong* — Carl Schurz, address to Anti-imperialistic Conference, Chicago, 1899; *A word fitly spoken* — Proverbs 15:11; *Small cheer and great welcome* — Shakespeare, *Comedy of Errors*

*Because of records destroyed in a fire, the author was unable to verify the source of this quotation.

6   High Mountains Are a Feeling

And the wooded sides of the mountain — Homer, the *Iliad*; . . . *as two grains of wheat* — Shakespeare, *The Merchant of Venice; A man may fall**; . . . *treasures in heaven* — Matthew 6:20; *Seven cities warred for Homer* — Thomas Heywood, *Hierarchy of the Blessed Angels; What is a man profited* — Matthew 16:26; *Verily the lust for comfort* — Kahlil Gibran, *The Prophet*; . . . *plain living and high thinking* — Wordsworth, sonnet; *What you wish you were* — Robert Jones Burdette*; . . . *ten thousands* — Beilby Porteus, *Death*; . . . *angling to be like the spirit of humility* — Izaak Walton, *The Compleat Angler*; . . . *calm, quiet, innocent recreation of angling* — Ibid; . . . *the stars inviting to slumber* — Virgil, the *Aeneid; As when the mind of man* — Ibid.; . . . *nothing that rises**; . . . *the hills, rock-ribbed and ancient* — William Cullen Bryant, "Thanatopsis"; . . . *the night's silence* — Rabindranath Tagore, *Stray Birds; We shall never understand one another* — Kahlil Gibran, *Sand and Foam; Let thy speech be better* — Dionysius the Elder*; *For we must look about* — Aristophanes, *The Trial of Euripides*; . . . *have often wondered how it is* — Marcus Aurelius Antoninus, *Meditations*

7   Now in September

The apples lie scattered everywhere — Virgil*; *Time hangs goldenly on now* — Gilean Douglas, "While Yet the Green Leaf"; *Ivies spring better* — Montaigne, "Of Experience"; *In nature's infinite book of secrecy* — Shakespeare, *Anthony and Cleopatra; O! mickle is the powerful grace* — Shakespeare, *Romeo and Juliet*; . . . *the glass of fashion* — Shakespeare, *Hamlet; Know you why the robin's breast* — Paul Hamilton Hayne, "Why the Robin's Breast Is Red"; . . . *Storied windows richly dight* — Milton, "Il Penseroso"; *Most of the social and political ills* — Plato, *The Republic; This people honoreth me with their lips* — Mark 7:6-9; *Cease to be ruled by dogmas* — Roger Bacon*; *The time of life is short* — Shakespeare, *King Henry IV*

8   End and Beginning

Go, and catch a falling star — John Donne, *Song; These are the days* — Emily Dickinson, No. 130; *There's rosemary and rue* — Shakespeare, *The Winter's Tale; For out of olde feldes* — Chaucer, *Parliament of Fowls; If any man has done wrong**; *I see the cloud-born squadrons* — Paul Hamilton Hayne, "A Storm in the Distance"; *That time of year* — Shakespeare, Sonnet 73; *How often we forget all time* — Byron, "The Island"; *He who ascends to mountain-tops* — Byron, *Childe Harold's Pilgrimage*

9   Wilderness Winter

Silence is the perfectest herald of joy — Shakespeare, *Much Ado About Nothing*; . . . *beauty is eternity* — Kahlil Gibran, *The Prophet; A good book is the precious life-blood* — Milton, "Areopagitica"; *And what is it to work with love?* — Kahlil Gibran, *The Prophet*; . . . *keep the word of promise to our ear* — Shakespeare, *Macbeth; The world is too much with us* — Wordsworth, "The World Is Too Much With Us"; *Where there is no vision* — Proverbs, 29:18; *Be silent now* — Gilean Douglas, "New Snow"; . . . *a snow year, a rich year* — George Herbert, *Jacula Prudentum; What is it to cease breathing* — Kahlil Gibran, *The Prophet; Give me my scallop-shell of quiet* — Sir Walter Raleigh, *The Passionate Man's Pilgrimage*

*Because of records destroyed in a fire, the author was unable to verify the source of this quotation.